THE CONTEMPORARY CARIBBEAN

CONTEMPORARY WORLDS explores the present and recent past. Books in the series take a distinctive theme, geo-political entity or cultural group and explore their developments over a period ranging usually over the last fifty years. The impact of current events and developments are accounted for by rapid but clear interpretation in order to unveil the cultural, political, religious and technological forces that are reshaping today's worlds.

SERIES EDITOR
Jeremy Black

In the same series

Britain since the Seventies
Jeremy Black

Sky Wars: A History of Military Aerospace Power
David Gates

War since 1945
Jeremy Black

The Global Economic System since 1945
Larry Allen

A Region in Turmoil:
South Asian Conflicts since 1947
Rob Johnson

Altered States:
America since the Sixties
Jeremy Black

THE CONTEMPORARY CARIBBEAN

History, Life and Culture since 1945

OLWYN M. BLOUET

REAKTION BOOKS

To my parents, Bertha and Lewis Salt, and to my brother, Jeff, who taught me to enjoy cricket, though rarely let me bat!

Published by Reaktion Books Ltd
33 Great Sutton Street
London EC1V 0DX
www.reaktionbooks.co.uk

First published 2007

Printed and bound in Great Britain
by Cromwell Press, Trowbridge, Wiltshire

British Library Cataloguing in Publication Data
Blouet, Olwyn M., 1948–
The contemporary Caribbean: history, life and culture since 1945. – (Contemporary worlds)
1. Caribbean Area – History – 1945–
I. Title
972.9'052

ISBN-13: 978 1 86189 313 0

Contents

Preface

This book has three objectives – to survey the Caribbean in a historical context; to describe the environmental, demographic, political, economic and cultural changes that have occurred since the end of World War II; and to present a profile of the characteristics that both unite and divide this multifaceted island territory.

Despite diverse colonial backgrounds, languages and cultures, the Caribbean islands share many environmental and historical characteristics, and face similar problems involving economic development, political stability and social cohesion. The small, open economies are vulnerable in the era of globalization, and island nations often struggle to maintain a sense of independence in a region overseen by the United States. But Caribbean people are adaptable and resilient. The greatest assets of the Caribbean are inventive and lively people and culture, which contribute a vigour and a vibrancy to the communities of the Atlantic world.

Introducing the Contemporary Caribbean

The contemporary Caribbean is a changing vision of blended histories and cultures. To affluent Europeans and North Americans the Caribbean most often appears as a tourist destination offering tropical beaches and warm sunsets. Tour operators project an image of paradise with sun, sand and sport. On the other hand, many Caribbean people leave the islands in search of jobs, education and economic opportunities in the United States, Canada and Europe.

The diverse and contrasting Caribbean worlds are marked by gulfs in access to wealth, education and global technology. There are rich and poor, employed and unemployed, literate and illiterate. Glitzy tourist enclaves and yachting marinas are at one end of the spectrum, shanty-towns and squalid slums at the other. Multinational companies, such as Dole, produce sugar and bananas for world markets, while small farmers struggle to grow subsistence crops on one or two acres. Globalization and the information age face localism, traditional lifestyles and poverty.

THE CARIBBEAN REGION

The Caribbean region is also called the Antilles or the West Indies. The term Caribbean is derived from the Caribs, a Native American group living on some of the islands when the Spaniards arrived in the late fifteenth century. Antilles is associated with 'Antilia', a mythical island believed to be in the Atlantic. French and Dutch speakers frequently use the term Antilles. The West Indies, used mostly in the Anglo-Caribbean, reflects the geographical mistake Columbus made when he believed he had reached Asia or 'the Indies'.

How do we define 'the Caribbean'? The islands are at the heart of the region, but surrounding areas share Caribbean coasts and similar historical and cultural characteristics. Recently there has been a tendency to expand the definition of the Caribbean. The geographer Gary Elbow distinguishes a 'core' Caribbean area of the Greater and Lesser Antilles. His 'fringe zone' includes the Bahamas, Belize (in Central America) and the Guyanas (in South America). The Caribbean coastal areas of Colombia, Venezuela, southern Mexico and Central America comprise Elbow's 'periphery'.[1] Other commentators consider South Florida to be in the Caribbean culture realm, with Miami as a regional capital. The *Miami Herald* acts as a regional newspaper.

The Caribbean islands are the focal point of this survey. Insularity has given them distinct histories, cultures, environments and identities. The islands were colonized by several European nations – Spain, the Netherlands, Britain and France – which gained early experiences with overseas expansion in the Caribbean. The densely populated islands have a history of sugar plantation agriculture based on enslaved African labour. They also share weak indigenous influences and a strong African heritage. Indentured workers coming from Asia in the nineteenth century added to the ethnic, cultural and religious diversity. Different languages, cultures and ethnicities coexist. Strategically, the islands have been, and continue to be, significant in terms of Atlantic trade and the security of the Americas.

Stretching more than 2,000 miles from the Bahamas in the north to Trinidad in the south, the Caribbean islands are usually divided into four geographical groups.[2]

The Greater Antilles includes the relatively large islands of Cuba, Hispaniola, Puerto Rico and Jamaica. Haiti and the Dominican Republic share the island of Hispaniola. Mountain ranges, part of a system that stretches from Central America, run in an east–west direction across the islands. Some of the mountains, like the Cordillera

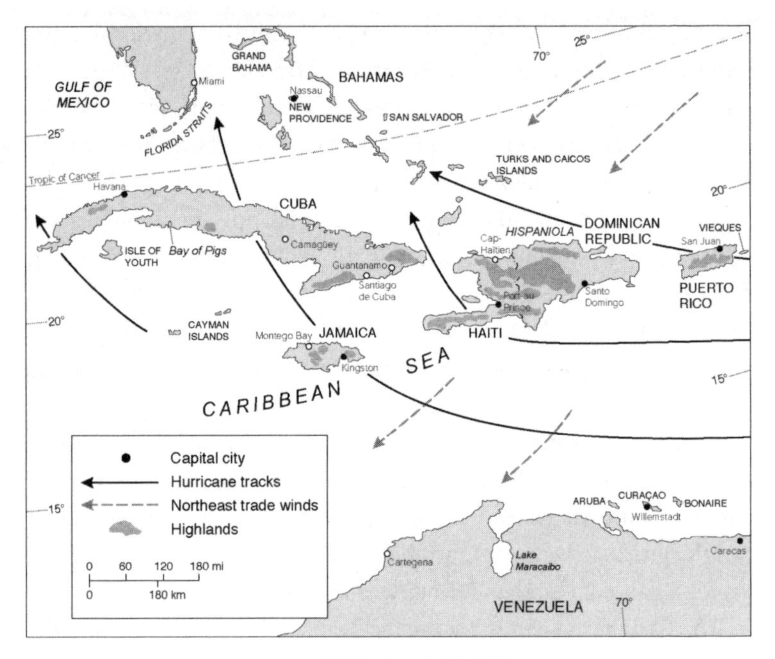

THE GREATER ANTILLES

Central on Hispaniola, contain gold and other minerals. The Greater Antilles has over 80 per cent of the land area of the islands, and about 90 per cent of Caribbean population. Spain, starting in 1492, established colonies in the islands of the Greater Antilles, including Jamaica. The larger islands offered the most in terms of precious metals and settled populations.

The Lesser Antilles is a group of smaller islands in the Eastern Caribbean made up of two arcs. In the inner arc, islands, such as St Kitts, Montserrat, part of Guadeloupe, Martinique and St Vincent, have formed around volcanoes. The outer arc is composed of low-lying limestone islands, such as Barbados, Antigua and St Martin. The Lesser Antilles were colonized by North Europeans, from Britain, France and the Netherlands, to gain footholds in the Western Atlantic world.

The South American offshore islands of Trinidad and Tobago, Aruba, Bonaire and Curaçao have more links to other Caribbean islands than to their neighbour, Venezuela, on the South American mainland. The ABC islands – Aruba, Bonaire and Curaçao – were colonized by the

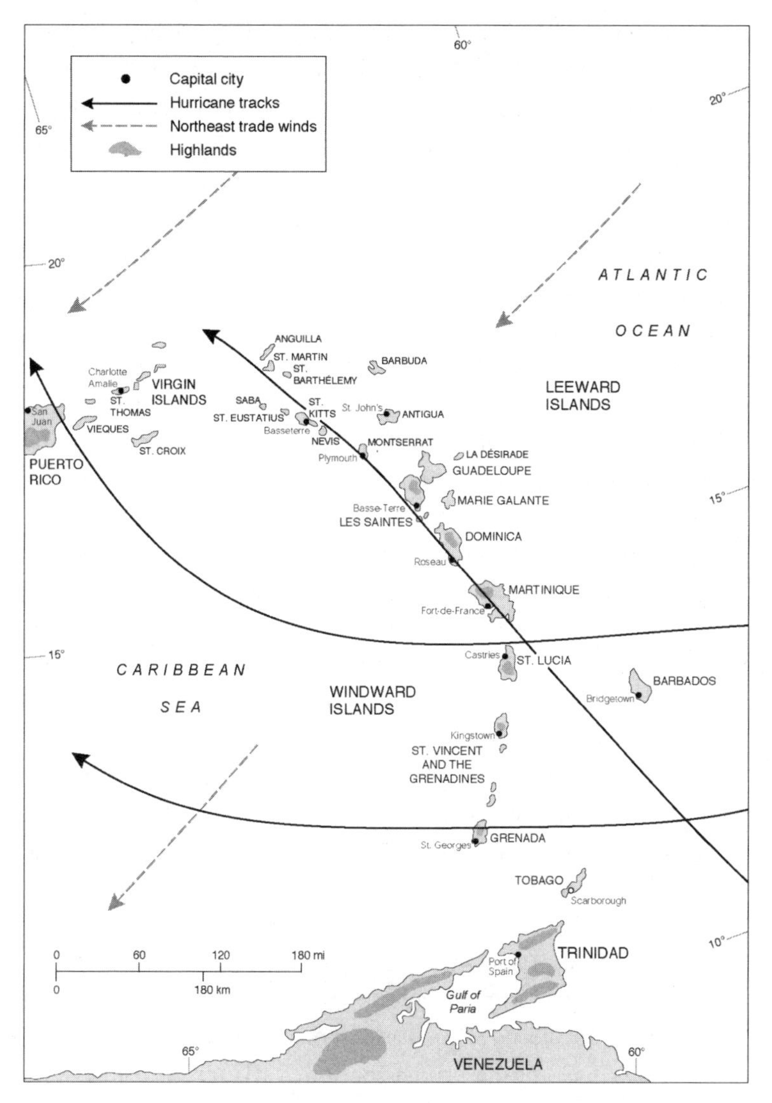

THE LESSER ANTILLES

Dutch for trade rather than for agriculture, since the soils of the islands are not fertile and rainfall is low. Trinidad, a minor Spanish colony, was taken by Britain in the Napoleonic Wars that ended in 1815. Geologically, Trinidad shares similarities with neighbouring South America, and was probably once connected to the mainland.

Off the coast of Florida, several hundred small, low-lying islands of porous limestone and coral make up the Bahamas group. There are more than 700 islands, many uninhabited. Some of the Bahama islands are north of the Tropic of Cancer (23.5°N) and not technically tropical lands. The Turks and Caicos Islands are included here and, like the Bahamas, are younger geologically than other islands in the Caribbean.

The contemporary Caribbean has significant Afro-Caribbean populations and shares elements of culture and creativity. The region of over 30 inhabited islands and a total population of nearly 40 million is diverse, made up of people speaking different languages, with a variety of cultural traditions and political systems (see Table 2). European colonization contributed to cultural diversity, although today the region is in the US sphere of influence.

Spain was the first to establish Caribbean colonies. Today the former Hispanic zone consists of Cuba, the Dominican Republic and Puerto Rico (see Table 1). Within the Spanish cultural area there is marked political diversity. Cuba, the largest Caribbean country (that includes numerous small islands), is under the control of Fidel Castro's communist regime. Puerto Rico has commonwealth status with the United States, and is arguably the largest remaining colony in the Caribbean. The Dominican Republic is trying to make democracy work, but has a political history of quasi-dictatorship and corruption.

The former British zone includes islands ranging from Jamaica, with a population of about 3 million, to Anguilla with several thousand. In the 1620s England began acquiring Caribbean colonies with St Kitts and Barbados. During the course of colonial warfare, the British took several islands from European powers, including Jamaica and Trinidad from Spain, and St Lucia and Grenada from France. Beginning in the 1960s many of the British-connected islands moved to independence, establishing parliamentary-style democracies. Today, only a few small islands, including Montserrat, Anguilla, the British Virgin Islands, the Caymans and the Turks and Caicos, are British Overseas Territories, with British citizenship rights.

The French colonial area includes Martinique, Guadeloupe and the northern part of St Martin. Today they are linked to France as Overseas Departments (Départements d'Outre Mer), with representation in the

Paris Assembly, and are included in the European Union. Haiti, which was controlled by France until slave revolution and independence in 1804, is the poorest country in the western hemisphere, and struggles to develop political and economic stability. Most Haitians are poor and speak a Creole language.

Six territories are connected to the Netherlands. St Eustatius, Saba, Bonaire and Curaçao comprise the Netherlands Antilles. Aruba and the southern part of St Martin are autonomous parts of the Kingdom of the Netherlands. All have status in the European Union.

The United States, although exerting influence in the entire contemporary Caribbean, has formal control only in Puerto Rico (acquired from Spain) and the US Virgin Islands of St Croix, St Thomas and St John, purchased from Denmark during World War I. People born in Puerto Rico and the US Virgin Islands are citizens of the United States.

Despite linguistic, cultural and political diversity, countries in the region share common historical themes and face similar challenges. The Caribbean has a history of conquest and colonialism. Native American peoples and cultures – Arawak, Taino and Carib – did not survive European conquest. Enslaved Africans were shipped across the Atlantic in the infamous slave trade, which increased once sugar developed as the major cash crop in the seventeenth century. For most islands sugar, slavery and plantation agriculture are part of the historical backdrop to the contemporary demographic and economic scene, which resulted in overpopulation and environmental degradation. Resistance is another theme running throughout the Caribbean: resistance to slavery, exploitation, colonialism, dependency and marginality.

Islands in the Caribbean encounter new challenges in the twenty-first century, as they seek to benefit from the changes associated with the developing global economy. Most islands are small, resource-poor and overpopulated in relation to jobs. Some islands, such as Trinidad with petroleum, Jamaica with bauxite and Cuba with nickel, have mineral resources and industrial sectors. But many islands, such as St Lucia and Grenada, rely on agricultural exports, like bananas, sugar, fruits and spices. More and more, tourism is the dominant economic activity and earner of foreign currency. Reliance on tourism means the region is as dependent on external forces as it always has been. Some commentators see tourism as the new monoculture that makes the islands vulnerable to the ups and downs of the North American and European economies.

Out-migration has been, and continues to be, a common response to economic vulnerability and fragility. Significant Caribbean communities are found in the United States, Canada and Europe. Migrants send home remittances to family members in the Caribbean that help local economies. In a geopolitical context, the Caribbean islands face dominance and interference from the United States, a country with a history of military and diplomatic intervention in the region.

Despite poverty problems and worries about economic viability in the global system, the Caribbean is a region of creativity and vitality. People are a valuable resource. In the islands there is a commitment to economic and social betterment. Many island governments strive for gender equity and racial equality. Out-migration is a response to continuing hardship and lack of jobs. But Caribbean people have had a lively impact on life outside the islands in Europe, North America and Central America. They have contributed labour and introduced Caribbean cuisine, music, celebrations, ideas and other assets into host countries, resulting in enrichment of all cultures. From calypso and carnival to Rastafarians and reggae, the Caribbean is an exciting world region with energy and zest.

Chapter 1

Geographical Setting and Environment

The Caribbean is a world of introduced peoples, plants and animals set in a tropical environment. Indigenous populations were decimated by European expansion, involving warfare, forced labour, social and economic disruption, and diseases. The region was colonized by Spain, Britain, France, the Netherlands and Denmark. Peoples from Europe, Africa and later Asia settled. Today the Caribbean islands are the most densely populated region of the Americas. Caribbean landscapes were transformed by intensive, tropical agriculture, as forests were cleared for crops. The nature of the environment was changed, as the risk of erosion and drought increased.[1]

Tourist brochures present the Caribbean as an environmental paradise of warm sun, soft sand and shimmering sea, but the region is subject to devastating natural hazards, including hurricanes, flooding, storm surges, volcanic eruptions, earthquakes, tsunamis and landslides.

HURRICANES

Hurricane Jeanne, the tenth named storm and fifth major hurricane of the 2004 Atlantic season, swept through the Caribbean territories of the US Virgin Islands, Puerto Rico, the Dominican Republic, Haiti and north-eastern Bahamas, before tracking to Florida. The government shut down the power grid in Puerto Rico as the storm approached, leaving 600,000 without electricity or running water. Landslides damaged the National Forest and seven people died. In the Dominican Republic most of the homes in the south-coast town of Samana were damaged and there were eighteen deaths. But Haiti, where weather-warning systems are poor, received the brunt of the hurricane, with 13 inches (33 cm) of rain resulting in flooding and mudslides in the Artibonite region, especially around the western coastal city of Gonaïves. Three thousand Haitians died and over 2,500 more were injured. Bodies were buried in mass graves to avoid the spread of disease.

Nearly all islands (with the possible exception of the ABC islands) face the threat of hurricanes that form between 5 and 20 degrees north and south of the Equator. Hurricanes generally move slowly westward across the Atlantic from the coast of Africa into the Caribbean Sea. In recent years they have occurred frequently, moving across the Atlantic into the Caribbean region from June until November, causing severe damage to people, property and crops. The name hurricane comes from the Native American term *hurakan*, or devil wind. Hurricanes develop from cells of low pressure that form over the Atlantic Ocean, generating strong winds that move anti-clockwise around a central 'eye'. Technically, a hurricane is recognized when a tropical storm picks up enough energy from the sea to generate winds over 74 miles per hour (119 kph). Torrential rain accompanies the high winds.

The Saffir-Simpson scale ranks hurricanes according to wind speed and storm surge as follows:

Category	Wind Speed (kph)	Storm Surge (metres)
1	119–153	1.2–1.5
2	154–177	1.8–2.4
3	178–209	2.7–3.6
4	210–249	3.9–5.5
5	over 249	over 5.5

Caribbean people live with an annual hurricane threat to farms, fields, homes and lives. Hurricane Jeanne in 2004 left approximately

3,000 dead in Haiti; Ivan, a category 4 hurricane, devastated Grenada in 2004, killing 29 and damaging about 85 per cent of the island. Ivan went on to cause death and destruction on Jamaica, Grand Cayman and Cuba. The Caribbean Development Bank estimates that Ivan cost $3 billion in damage. Hurricane Dennis hit early in 2005, killing several people in Cuba and Haiti. In October 2005 Wilma struck the north-west coast of Cuba and breached the sea defences of Havana, leaving hundreds homeless.

Nowadays deaths are minimized because of better warning systems, but hurricane disasters always involve loss of power and water services, damage to housing (particularly roofs) and destruction of agricultural crops. Hurricanes are accompanied by storm surges, causing coastal flooding and beach erosion. High rainfall exacerbates flooding. As we have seen when hurricane Katrina impacted New Orleans and the US Gulf coast in 2005, the poorest in society are the least able to cope with hurricane damage, partly because they do not have the resources to evacuate and partly because they are more likely to live in low-lying, flood-prone areas that the better-off leave vacant.

The World Meteorological Organization names Atlantic hurricanes alphabetically. In 2005, for the first time on record, all 26 letters of the alphabet were used before going to the Greek alphabet. Some experts believe that, because of global warming and a rise in sea-surface temperatures, hurricanes will be more common and more severe in the coming years.

Locals in the Caribbean sometimes use humour in an attempt to demystify and cope with the annual experience of hurricanes. The most famous example was by Lloyd Lovindeer, a Jamaican songwriter who poked fun at 'Wild Gilbert', the 1988 hurricane that crossed over Jamaica as a category 4 hurricane, killing 45 in Jamaica and 30 in Haiti before moving on to Grand Cayman and the Yucatán Peninsula. He sang:

> ... The little dog laughed to see such fun,
> And the dish ran away with the spoon.
> Oona seen me dish, oona seen me dish,
> Anybody, oona seen me satellite dish?

Dish take off like flying-saucer.
Me roof migrate without a visa . . .
One cold beer cost ten dollar.[2]

Here are references to several Caribbean themes, including the use of old English nursery rhymes (reflecting the colonial past), satellite dishes and links to the global information age, migration (whether documented or not) as a fact of everyday life, and the high cost of consumer goods, especially in a crisis.

EARTHQUAKES AND VOLCANOES

The geological structure of the region means that the Caribbean is not only subject to major hurricanes, but earthquake and volcanic activity as well. The American and Caribbean tectonic plates rub against each other, stresses build up along fault lines, and the result is earthquakes and, in some places, active volcanoes. All islands are subject to earthquakes, which are measured on the Richter scale. Each number on the scale is ten times more powerful that the number below it; that is, a quake measuring 7.0 is ten times greater than one rated 6.0. The best-known earthquake in the region occurred in 1692, and destroyed Port Royal, Jamaica, a notorious pirate base. Kingston was established as the new capital, but it too suffered a quake in 1907, followed by a devastating fire. Parts of the Dominican Republic and Puerto Rico, close to a deep underwater trough, are particularly susceptible to earthquakes. Puerto Rico experienced major disasters in 1670, 1787, 1867 and 1918.[3]

Active volcanoes are confined to an inner island arc running north from Grenada to St Kitts. Mt Soufrière on Guadeloupe is the highest volcanic peak in the Lesser Antilles at 1,467 metres. The volcano erupted in 1976 but no one was killed, thanks to effective evacuation. The most devastating eruption was in 1902 when Mt Pelée exploded on Martinique, killing an estimated 30,000 people and completely destroying the town of St Pierre. In 1979 Mt Soufrière on St Vincent erupted. Since 1995 Montserrat has suffered volcanic activity and eruptions from the Soufrière Hills Volcano. About two-thirds of the island, including the former capital of Plymouth, is uninhabitable, and many residents have been evacuated to other islands or Britain. St Vincent and St Kitts are classified as high-risk islands for future volcanic activity.[4] St Lucia has the picturesque Twin Pitons, extinct volcanic plugs, now a World Heritage Site and a major tourist attraction.

Undersea earthquakes can set the sea in motion, resulting in waves of water (tsunamis) that can wreak intense devastation and loss of life, as we know from the traumatic East Asian tsunami of Boxing Day (26 December) 2004. The most recent tsunami in the Caribbean affected the Dominican Republic in 1946.

FLOODS AND LANDSLIDES

Flooding is the most common hazard in the Caribbean. Hurricanes and tropical storms frequently result in flood conditions, but slower moving depressions can also cause severe flooding. Landslides can accompany heavy rainfall, and are also caused by earthquake activity. Sometimes humans exacerbate landslide potential by removing forest cover and vegetation, or by building on slopes and adding weight to hillsides. Again, poorer members of societies often live in areas most prone to floods and landslides, and are the least able to handle the catastrophes.

CONTEMPORARY RESPONSES TO NATURAL HAZARDS

Natural hazards can create human, social and economic disasters. Some disasters even have political repercussions. Most countries in the Caribbean have tried to develop disaster planning and hazard management agendas. Strategies involve data collection and analysis to help with mapping and assessment of potential danger. Modern technology provides better warning and preparedness systems, the most obvious example being satellite imagery that allows the path of hurricanes to be forecast in the Caribbean islands. The Caribbean Disaster Emergency Response Agency (CDERA) currently seeks to inform and educate governments and NGOs (non-governmental organizations), minimize disaster impact and coordinate relief among the sixteen states involved in the agency. Researchers at the University of the West Indies also analyse information and run workshops to assist with disaster management, mitigation and education.

The impact of natural hazards can be reduced by active strategies, some of which are difficult to enforce. For example, land-use planning and zoning can attempt to prevent building in high-risk areas for earthquakes, landslides and flooding. Better designed and engineered buildings, although expensive, can reduce the impact of hurricanes and earthquakes. Unfortunately, despite progress in recent years, much remains to be accomplished. Growing population numbers and urbanization do not help the situation. Often rural to urban migrants live in squatter settlements on marginal land prone to flooding and environmental hazards.

CLIMATE AND LANDSCAPES

The Caribbean islands experience a maritime tropical climate with high humidity, although the Bahamas and northern areas of Cuba and Jamaica can have cold air penetrating from the north in winter, bringing heavy rain. Average temperatures are around 80° F (26.7° C) with little temperature variation throughout the year. In fact, daily temperature ranges are greater than seasonal ranges. Temperatures are modified by height, so that some of the mountainous areas of the Greater Antilles experience cold temperatures and even frost on high peaks, as in the Dominican Republic. Tropical heat is also modified by the north-east trade winds that bring considerable rainfall. There are marked wet and dry seasons, with more rain falling in the summer months. December to April is the drier period, a time when tourist prices peak. Traditionally, sugar cane was, and still is, harvested during these months.

Island climates vary significantly. Generally speaking, low-lying islands receive less rain than those with mountainous regions. For example, off the coast of Venezuela, the flat ABC islands – Aruba,

Bonaire and Curaçao – get an average of only 20 inches (51 cm) of rain per year, and have a semi-arid vegetation of scrub, aloes and cacti. Islands that have high peaks receive over 100 inches (254 cm) of rain per annum in certain areas. Central parts of Dominica, for example, receive well over 100 inches a year and can support abundant areas of rainforest. The higher the elevation, the cooler and wetter it becomes.

The major rain-makers (excluding hurricanes) are the north-east trade winds that blow across the Caribbean, bringing unstable air full of moisture. Rainfall variation within islands is a result of what is known as orographic rainfall, when moisture-laden air from the trade winds rises over high ground and cools to produce precipitation on the windward slopes. Some areas on the drier, leeward (south-west) side of islands are in a rain-shadow zone and receive significantly lower rainfall totals than areas on the north-east slopes. For example, Montego Bay on the north coast of Jamaica gets an average of 51.26 inches (130 cm) of rain per year, but Kingston on the south coast only receives 31.4 inches (80 cm) per annum. Many coastal locations away from higher ground receive little rain. The northern part of Puerto Rico is relatively lush when compared to dry areas in the south. Low-lying islands such as Antigua and the ABC islands receive little rainfall and drought is common. Houses frequently have water cisterns for domestic water collection.

Rainfall also results from convection. The land heats and generates upward convectional air currents, leading to condensation and precipitation. Typically, clouds build up during the day and by mid- to late afternoon large cumulo-nimbus clouds form, producing thunderous downpours.

Most of the mature native forests have disappeared since the time of European colonization because of clearance for agriculture, especially sugar cane. Timber was used for construction, fences, and to fuel boiling houses for sugar production. In the Lesser Antilles this process, beginning in the seventeenth century, has been referred to as the 'great clearing'.[5] In Cuba, although destruction of hard-wood forests in the west and central regions came later in the nineteenth century, the process was similar and has been called the 'death of the forest'.[6] In the twentieth century Cuban forests in the east were cut down to make way for US sugar interests. Thousands of acres in the Dominican Republic were similarly destroyed to clear land for sugar cane.[7]

Primary rainforests, such as El Yunque in Puerto Rico, remain in upland areas. Dominica has significant areas of verdant rainforest. Turners Hall Wood in Barbados survives as a small native woodland amidst land cleared for sugar cultivation. There are still significant areas of forest in dry limestone country in Cuba, the Dominican Republic and Puerto Rico. The core of the Cockpit Country in Jamaica is a forest reserve. Some islands, such as Antigua, have no forest cover today. Haiti, once heavily forested, has suffered badly from deforestation and erosion, and little land is now forest.

Some Caribbean islands have significant mountain peaks. Pico Duarte, at 10,417 feet (3,175 m), in the Dominican Republic is the highest. Areas of the Central Highlands in the Dominican Republic, referred to as 'little Switzerland', can get frost in winter, and the region is popular with Dominicans because of its cooler climate. However, the Caribbean region is best known for coastal environments. Beaches are crucial to the appeal of the Caribbean for tourists and island economies. But beaches are under threat from pollution, linked to industrialization, urbanization, natural hazards and tourism. Tourists, their hotels, cruise-ships and activities, all lead to increased pollution, environmental problems and beach erosion. Coral reefs are threatened by environmental degradation. The Caribbean is home to 14 per cent of the world's coral reefs, with the reefs of the Bahamas platform being the most extensive.[8] Reefs have to be conserved because they function as breakwaters to help protect beaches, are nurseries for fish, and, of course, act as tourist magnets. Mangrove and wetland areas, which have been frequently drained for building purposes, also need to be protected, not only for aesthetic reasons, but also because they help to protect environments from hurricane and flood damage. Today, because more is known about the importance of these areas to the whole coastal ecosystems, some governments are protecting wetlands; the Nariva Swamp in Trinidad, for example, is now a national park. But more needs to be done to protect fragile environments.

Flora and fauna are also threatened by habitat destruction and commercial activity. The Caribbean islands are home to numerous species of plants and animals not found elsewhere in the world. St Lucia has a distinct type of parrot, as does St Vincent. Dominica has two unique parrot species. Over 40 species of butterfly are found on Hispaniola (today's Haiti and Dominican Republic) and nowhere else. The Caribbean islands lie on a route between North and South America and are visited by many migratory birds. Species extinction is a threat, and numerous plants and animals have become extinct in the last century, but some island governments are trying to take action. For instance, Jamaica has a Wildlife Protection Act that seeks to safeguard animals, including several types of turtle, the Jamaican iguana, the manatee, the American crocodile and two species of parrot.[9]

SUSTAINABLE DEVELOPMENT

Environmental issues are currently attracting more attention in Caribbean political and public circles. There is an interest in sustainable development which recognizes that environments are fragile and have to be nurtured for future generations. Sustainable development involves maintaining biological diversity and protecting natural habitats on land and at sea, while preventing pollution and environmental degradation. It involves foregoing short-term gains in favour of long-term environmental goals. The concept also incorporates the idea of encouraging social and economic development for all in the community.

Many Caribbean countries are signing on to international conventions relating to environmental protection. A good example is the Convention on Biological Diversity, introduced at the Earth Summit in Rio de Janeiro in 1992. Most Caribbean countries, including St Kitts, Nevis, St Lucia, the Bahamas, Barbados, Cuba, Dominica, Grenada and Jamaica, are signatories.

Governments have begun to conserve native flora and fauna in national parks and protected areas on land and sea. Dominica, for example, has the Morne Trois Pitons Rainforest National Park, which preserves the environment and promotes eco-tourism. Cuba has a well-organized government system of protected areas, including the Humboldt National Park, a World Heritage Site. Some commentators suggest that the most effective way to achieve environmental preservation is to encourage cooperation between governments and local people. In many areas much remains to be done to make sustainable development a reality, but awareness of the fragility of the landscape and wildlife has begun.

Many in the scientific world are concerned about the impact of 'global warming', whatever the cause. If global warming continues, potential consequences for the Caribbean include rising sea levels (bringing coastal flooding), coral bleaching and more severe weather events, especially hurricanes, due to warmer sea temperatures. Some commentators believe that the international community should act promptly to curb greenhouse emissions or we could reach a point of no return.

ENVIRONMENTAL CONTRASTS: HAITI AND THE DOMINICAN REPUBLIC

According to early Spanish accounts, the island of Hispaniola was mostly forested at the time of Encounter in the 1490s. Today in Hispaniola there are large environmental differences between the eastern third, Haiti, and the western two-thirds, the Dominican Republic. Haiti is almost treeless but about one quarter of the Dominican Republic is forested.[10] Viewed from an aerial photograph the border area between Haiti and the Dominican Republic reveals a marked contrast in forest cover. Because of extreme deforestation Haiti suffers from soil erosion, loss of watershed protection, excess sediment in rivers, decreased rainfall and shortage of wood for fuel. Haiti, the poorest country in the Americas, is overpopulated and most people are subsistence farmers. By contrast, the Dominican Republic has fewer environmental problems, less population pressure and a more developed economy. Per capita income is higher in the Dominican Republic than in Haiti.

Sharing the same island, and with shared histories of colonialism and US occupation, why have the two countries developed differently? There are some natural environmental variables. Generally speaking the Dominican Republic receives more rainfall than Haiti, because much of the Haitian side of the island is screened by mountains and in a rain-shadow area. The Dominican Republic has areas of thick, rich soil, such as the Cibao Valley, that are especially fertile.

But more important are the historical, economic, social and political developments. Haiti (known as St Domingue) was French, the Dominican Republic Spanish. The French invested in sugar plantation agriculture; Spain, in decline during the seventeenth and eighteenth centuries, continued low intensive land use of mixed farming and ranching. Haiti imported tens of thousands of enslaved Africans, the Dominican Republic considerably fewer. By the 1780s St Domingue was the richest colony in the Americas, before the massive slave rebellion (the Haitian Revolution) led to independence from France in 1804, when sugar plantations were devastated and ex-slaves farmed small plots on any available land. Forest cover was destroyed as peasants cleared land for coffee and subsistence crops, and used wood for building and as fuel for cooking. The Dominican Republic did develop export agriculture involving tobacco, coffee, cacao and, after the 1870s, sugar cane. But it was a later development; the slave trade was over; and there was not as much population pressure on resources in the Dominican Republic.

A further important factor is that environmental protection policies have been relatively successful in the Dominican Republic. Beginning in the early 1900s grass-roots pressure led to the first natural reserve, the Vedado del Yaque, near Santiago. The dictator Rafael Trujillo (1930–1961), partly because he wanted to control logging for his own benefit and partly to protect watersheds, established national parks, created conservation areas and limited the burning of forest for agriculture. He owned large pine forests, but his logging activities left some tree stands as a seed source for new growth. After his assassination logging increased until President Balaguer banned commercial logging and turned enforcement over to the military, who were not afraid to use force. Squatters and rich home-owners were ejected from national parks. People were encouraged to use subsidized liquefied natural gas rather than charcoal. In the 1960s and '70s strong-man Joaquín Balaguer had an impressive environmental record. He expanded the natural reserve system, established two coastal national parks, added two underwater whale sanctuaries and taxed mining companies. He started an aquarium, a botanical garden and a Natural History Museum.

Today the Dominican government teams up with universities and NGOs to conserve environmental resources. All is not perfect. The Dominican Republic suffers from damage to coastlines and fisheries, and from soil erosion and poor water quality. But there are over 70 reserves covering a considerable proportion of land. Dominicans have an impressive environmental record for a relatively poor country.[11] Meanwhile, Haiti becomes more overpopulated and poorer, with little hope for a healthy future.

Chapter 2

History to 1945

The contemporary Caribbean has been shaped by colonialism, sugar plantation agriculture and slavery. The Caribbean islands were transformed into a region of introduced people, plants and animals, and became involved in a growing Atlantic world linking Africa, the Americas and Europe. African labour, Caribbean land and European capital produced agricultural commodities (principally sugar) for export to Europe. External political and economic control, and export of profits, were the rule. The result is a large Afro-Caribbean population, a story of struggle, survival and resilience, a desire for political independence, and a commitment to social and economic well-being.

EARLY HISTORY

Before the first voyage of Christopher Columbus in 1492, the Caribbean islands were inhabited by three Native American groups, which had originally migrated from the South American mainland. The Ciboney, who relied on fishing, hunting and gathering, lived in western Cuba and south-west Hispaniola. Taino-Arawak people, who had migrated from South America in canoes, dominated the Greater Antilles, where Hispaniola was the most populated island at the time of European contact. The Taino-Arawaks practised agriculture, growing root crops, including manioc (also known as cassava), sweet potatoes and peanuts on plots that had been cleared by 'slash and burn' practices. Soil was mounded into permanent raised fields (*conucos*). Bitter manioc is poisonous if not properly prepared, but it stores well, is resistant to pests, and is high in calories. The Arawaks also grew maize, beans and other crops, including tobacco, which they smoked. They may have used irrigation canals in Cuba and Southern Hispaniola. Their agricultural system was efficient and productive, and was not harsh on the land. Animal protein was provided by hunting and fishing. Cotton was used for dress, fishnets and hammocks. Pottery and baskets were produced, and gold was worked into jewellery. But technology did not include the wheel, iron tools or writing.

Estimates of Native American population numbers at the time of Encounter vary greatly. The contemporary Dominican friar Bartolomé de Las Casas estimated that there were 3 million people on Hispaniola alone. Las Casas recorded cruel abuses against Indians and became their protector. He claimed that Native American leaders were slow-roasted by the Spanish. One condemned chief, when asked by a priest to embrace Christianity and go to heaven, replied that he would rather go to hell![1] Many scholars accept a pre-contact figure of about 1 million for the entire Caribbean. We do know that the numbers dropped drastically and rapidly after contact with Spaniards. By about 1570 the Arawak, as a separate people, had disappeared in the Greater Antilles due to Spanish expansion, warfare, harsh treatment, slavery, social disruption and the spread of 'Old World' diseases, including smallpox, influenza, measles and malaria, against which they lacked immunity. Arawaks may have passed cultural traits to the Spaniards and Africans, particularly in agriculture.

The Caribs, who gave their name to the region, were principally in the Lesser Antilles, and were raiding Puerto Rico at the time of the Spanish advance. Because of initial effective resistance the Caribs slowed European penetration, and held out longer than the Arawaks. It appears that the Caribs relied more on hunting, gathering and fishing, although they did practise some agriculture. It was reported that they ate the flesh of enemies, and so they are associated with cannibalism. Eventually the North Europeans took over in the Lesser Antilles after episodes of fierce fighting. Today a few remaining Caribs live in St

Vincent and Dominica, and some black Caribs are in Belize, forcibly moved from the islands by the British colonial government after resistance in the late eighteenth century.

Columbus's attempt to reach Asia by sailing westwards from Europe radically changed the face of the Caribbean world. Columbus, a good mariner but poor geographer, severely underestimated the westward distance from Europe to Asia when he set out with three ships, the *Niña*, *Pinta* and *Santa Maria*, in 1492. The voyage was financed by King Ferdinand and Queen Isabella of Spain. Columbus was trying to find a direct sea route to Asia that would cut out the Muslim merchants who controlled the trade. He first landed in San Salvador in the Bahamas, before moving on to explore the northern coasts of Cuba and Hispaniola. Columbus believed he was in Asia (the Indies), hence the name West Indies. A few settlers were left at Navidad on the north coast of Hispaniola, but did not survive.

The second voyage in 1493, a much larger affair than the first, was an attempt to establish an agricultural and mining colony on Hispaniola that would act as a base for expeditions to India. It was on this voyage that sugar cane was first taken to the Americas. A settlement was established at La Isabela on the north coast of Hispaniola, but colonists faced problems with food supplies and the Native Americans, even though there was some gold to be had. Columbus had difficulty managing the greedy settlers, and in 1496 returned to Spain. He was back in the Caribbean two years later, landing at the newly established town of Santo Domingo on the south coast, a much more promising site. Santo Domingo was the first successful Spanish urban area in the Americas and became the administrative centre of the islands and the whole of New Spain (which later included Mexico) for a time. Santo Domingo was so important that its name was used for the entire Spanish colony. Today it is the capital of the Dominican Republic, a city of over 1 million people, with plaza, government buildings, cathedral (started in 1514) and university. Eventually Columbus was sent back to Spain in disgrace, accused of being a tyrant, but the islands he had stumbled upon would never be the same, nor would the world.

Spanish explorers quickly surveyed the Greater Antilles in search of precious metals and resources. Settlements spread out from

Hispaniola to Jamaica, Cuba and Puerto Rico. Gold was found in Hispaniola, Puerto Rico and Cuba, but output peaked by about 1520 and declined. Indians on all the islands were forced to work in farming and mining in a slavery -like arrangement that led to many deaths.

The Caribbean islands were the focus of Spanish imperial attention until 1519–21, when the Hernán Cortés expedition sailed from Cuba, subdued the Aztec Empire and shifted interest to the American mainland. Mexico City was built on the ruins of the large Aztec capital, Tenochtitlán, which had been a Native American city of perhaps 200,000 inhabitants – larger than contemporary Seville, Paris or London. The Zacatecas silver deposits, north of Mexico City, were discovered in the 1540s, helping to finance the Golden Age of Spain in the sixteenth century, before inflation and decline followed.

The Pizarro brothers led the way for penetration of South America after defeating the Incas, centred in Peru, in 1532–3. Subsequently, in the 1540s, rich silver deposits were found at Potosí, in the heart of the Inca Empire. By that time the Native populations of the Greater Antilles had been decimated, especially after a smallpox epidemic hit Hispaniola in 1518, the same year the Atlantic slave trade gained Spanish royal approval. Enslaved Africans, bought along the coast of West Africa, were shipped to the Caribbean as a vital labour source.

The Greater Antilles became staging posts and supply bases, providing foodstuffs, cattle, hides and tallow for penetration of the mainland (the Vice-royalties of New Spain and Peru). The Spaniards introduced sugar cane, citrus, coffee and bananas, later to be significant crops in the context of Caribbean export agriculture. Wheat, olives and vines also moved from the 'Old World' to the 'New', but did not do well in Caribbean island environments. Cattle, horses, mules, pigs, sheep and goats were introduced to the Americas from Europe. Cattle and pigs had a destructive impact on Caribbean environments, since the Spaniards left these animals on islands to breed as a ready food source. Tobacco, an important native American crop, was grown and exported to Europe. Sugar was shipped to Spain from Hispaniola starting in the 1520s, but was not as significant as it would later become, due to transportation problems and a labour shortage.[2] Maize, originally domesticated in Middle America, and potatoes, originally domesticated in the Andes, would become important crops in Europe and elsewhere. This 'Columbian Exchange' of plants and animals changed agriculture and food practices around the world.

The sixteenth century was the Spanish century in the Caribbean. Spanish merchants operated under a strict government-controlled system known as mercantilism, which was the opposite of free trade. Tariffs were high, monopolies common, and goods moved in Spanish ships. Not surprisingly, other merchants wanted to trade in the Caribbean. Interlopers and pirates from England, France and the Netherlands made a nuisance of themselves in the Atlantic and Caribbean Sea, illegally trading with Spanish colonies and sometimes attacking Spanish shipping, especially the silver *flotas* (convoys). Towns such as Havana, on the important shipping route through the Florida Straits, became targets for pirates. The Spanish found it necessary to build impressive fortifications to protect harbours. Today fortifications are tourist attractions at San Juan, Santo Domingo, Havana, Cartagena (Colombia) and St Augustine in Florida.

Two of the most infamous privateers were John Hawkins (1532–1595) and Francis Drake (1540–1596), both from Plymouth and both supported by Queen Elizabeth I. Hawkins traded with the Spanish and sold slaves from West Africa to Spanish settlers in the Caribbean. Drake, the first Englishman to sail around the world (1577–80), attacked Spanish towns and shipping regularly, most famously in 1572 when he invaded Nombre de Dios, capturing a load of silver en route from South America. Hawkins and Drake were leaders in the defeat of the Spanish Armada (1588) and in 1595 were financed by Elizabeth I to attack Spanish interests in Panama and the Caribbean. The expedition was unsuccessful. Hawkins died off Puerto Rico in 1595 and Drake died at sea near Portobello the following year.

THE SEVENTEENTH CENTURY

In the seventeenth century the North Europeans – the Dutch, English and French – established colonies in the Lesser Antilles. The Dutch West India Company, chartered in 1621, was given a monopoly on

Dutch trade along the coasts of America and Africa. Thanks to successful Dutch attacks on Spanish shipping, other countries were able to penetrate the Caribbean and acquire colonies. The Dutch favoured trading and smuggling bases, such as Curaçao (also an important salt source for the Dutch fishing industry) and St Eustatius. In the first half of the seventeenth century the Dutch also controlled the sugar producing region of north-east Brazil, including Pernambuco, that they had taken from Portugal.

In the 1620s and '30s, after unsuccessful attempts in St Lucia and Grenada, the English colonized part of St Kitts, Nevis, Barbados, Antigua and Montserrat. The English used joint-stock companies, financed by investors, to fund colonial projects. Investors expected profits. Initially white settlers, some free and some indentured servants, grew crops such as tobacco, cotton, indigo (a blue dye) and ginger for export to Europe. In the 1640s sugar became the most profitable crop because it was in demand, commanded a high price and, unlike tobacco, could only be grown in the tropics and sub-tropics. Tobacco, grown in non-tropical environments such as Virginia and Maryland, was overproduced and suffered depressed prices in the 1630s and '40s. The French, encouraged by the mercantilist policies of Cardinal Richelieu and Jean-Baptiste Colbert, settled on Martinique, Guadeloupe and part of St Kitts, where the shift to sugar production was slower than in the English islands, possibly because of a labour shortage.

The 'Sugar Revolution' – a shift to sugar plantations and slave labour – began in Barbados in the 1640s, with Dutch assistance, know-how and credit. In the Caribbean islands sugar production involved three operations at the plantation – growing and harvesting sugar cane, crushing cane to extract juice, and boiling juice to crystallize sugar. Additional refining occurred in Europe. The growing and manufacture of sugar soon spread from Barbados to other islands in the Lesser Antilles. In the seventeenth century Barbados produced the most wealth of the British colonial system, surpassing Virginia and Massachusetts. Bridgetown, the capital of Barbados, was one of the busiest ports in the North Atlantic. Many white Barbadians, lacking land and capital to shift to sugar, migrated to North American colonies (especially South Carolina) to acquire land. As supplies of white indentured labourers dropped, more and more slaves were imported from Africa to work the sugar plantations. A demographic transformation created large black majorities in the English and French islands.

Spanish ascendancy in the Caribbean was challenged by the growing power of England and France during the second half of the seventeenth century. Spain lost Jamaica to England in the 1650s as a result of Oliver Cromwell's 'Western Design' – originally a failed scheme to capture Hispaniola. Jamaica was taken as a consolation prize. By the Treaty of Ryswick in 1697 France took formal control of Western Hispaniola, calling it St Domingue, later to be renamed Haiti at independence in 1804. Planters in Jamaica and St Domingue developed intensive sugar plantation agriculture in the early 1700s. Labour was provided by large numbers of enslaved Africans, who survived the 'Middle Passage' of the so-called Triangular Trade that linked Europe, Africa and the Americas. However, not all ships sailed all three legs of the route. Specialized slave vessels went back and forth between Africa and the Americas. In addition, there was sea-borne trade between North America and the West Indies, supplying grain, fish and lumber to the islands, and sugar, molasses and rum to the mainland.

THE EIGHTEENTH CENTURY

Sugar and Slavery

In the eighteenth century sugar production in the British and French Caribbean colonies expanded and peaked. Demand for sugar rose substantially, especially in Britain, where it was associated with improved living standards and increased consumption of tea and coffee. The sugar industry needed large labour supplies, especially at harvest time, when cane had to be cut, carted, crushed and the juice boiled expeditiously to crystallize the sugar. During the sugar harvest boiling houses operated around the clock. Africa supplied the necessary labour force. It is estimated that, of the roughly 10 to 12 million enslaved Africans imported into the Americas during the period of the Atlantic slave trade, over 3.2 million (the vast majority imported during the eighteenth century) arrived in the British and French Caribbean islands from the west coast of Africa.[3] Slave death rates were high and birth rates low. Because there was no natural increase of slaves in the British and French islands (caused by many factors, including harsh labour, food deficits, unequal sex ratios and disease), continuous slave imports were needed. London, Bristol and Liverpool were heavily involved in the eighteenth-century slave trade, and French slavers operated out of Bordeaux and Nantes. Slaves were generally supplied by African merchants on the African coast, and exchanged for commodities such as textiles, guns, trinkets and gin. Some historians, including Eric Williams, a former Prime Minister of Trinidad, argue that the slave trade and sugar economies of the Caribbean developed capitalism and the Industrial Revolution on the backs of slaves.[4]

In addition to labour, Africans contributed rich cultural traits to the Caribbean, including music, dance, belief systems and folk tales, as well as agricultural, medical and handicraft skills. Food plants such as rice, okra, black-eyed peas, ackee fruit, yams, millet and sorghum were taken from Africa to the Americas.[5] The islands display many African traits, modified by Creole adaptations and modern creations. To many commentators, African background and lifestyle patterns are keys to understanding and appreciating major aspects of Caribbean culture.

Slavery was always resisted by the enslaved, with frequent outbreaks of rebellion and violence. Some slaves fled to freedom, establishing maroon communities in the interiors of islands, such as the Cockpit Country of Jamaica. The word maroon is derived from *cimarrone*, meaning 'dweller of the summits', originally Native Americans who fled from the Spaniards into the interiors of islands and were later joined by runaway slaves.

Towards the end of the eighteenth century the slave trade and the institution of slavery began to be challenged by politicians and humanitarians. In England the Society for the Abolition of Slavery, with William Pitt and William Wilberforce heavily involved, was organized in the 1780s. The Society first attacked the slave trade then slave ownership. In the nineteenth century the Atlantic slave trade and the institution of slavery would come to an end in the Caribbean.

Warfare

The eighteenth century was a period of intense international competition and warfare, with France against Britain in conflict over colonies and trade. Both countries operated mercantilist economic policies involving monopolies and trade restrictions, and both were engaged in fierce competition for markets and profits. Wars that had European and colonial contexts included the War of Spanish Succession (1701–14), the War of Jenkins' Ear between Britain and Spain (1739), the War of Austrian Succession (1740–48) and the Seven Years War (1756–63), also known as the French and Indian War. When war broke out in Europe or the colonies it was frequently accompanied by naval operations in the Caribbean. As a result of numerous confrontations several Caribbean colonies changed hands many times. St Lucia, important for the defence of Martinique, was held by France nine times and by Britain six times![6] British control was continuous after the Napoleonic Wars (1793–1815), until St Lucian independence in 1979. Tobago was another island fiercely contested by France and Britain during the eighteenth century. In 1888 Tobago was jointly administered with Trinidad, although there is still a lot of Tobagan pride and sense of difference.

The Seven Years War – a truly global encounter with conflict in Europe, the Americas and Asia – was a pivotal event in the Atlantic world. After heavy fighting in the Caribbean and North America (including Canada), France was eventually defeated by the British, who surprised even Spain by capturing Havana towards the end of the war. At the concluding Treaty of Paris (1763) British officials debated whether to hold on to the small French sugar island of Guadeloupe or the large French territory in Canada. Canada was retained but only after discussion, illustrating the significance of sugar islands in the international mindset of the eighteenth century. Britain also annexed Dominica, St Vincent, Grenada and Tobago (the so-called ceded islands) in 1763.

The Seven Years War was followed by a tumultuous age of revolutions, including the American Revolution, French Revolution, Haitian Revolution and Revolutionary Wars of Independence in Latin America.

The American Revolution (1776–83) had a severe impact on the Caribbean, where fighting broke out between Britain and France, because France was helping the rebellious American colonists. Britain found it difficult to defend its Caribbean possessions when the fleet was needed on the east coast of North America. Many islands, including St Kitts, Nevis and Montserrat, were taken by French forces. The sugar trade was disrupted by naval operations. There were food shortages, and some starvation deaths, because few provisions came from places like South Carolina (rice) and Virginia (grain). Many planters and merchants in the British Caribbean were sympathetic to the American cause, equally resenting high taxes and trade controls, but the difference was that the islands needed the British military for defence against the French and in case of slave rebellion. At the end of the conflict in 1783 most islands were returned to the original colonial power. With American independence, however, the islands lost preferential trade in foodstuffs and supplies from the thirteen colonies, and suffered hardship.[7]

The French Revolution, which began in 1789 with the fall of the Bastille, sparked turmoil in St Domingue, as first free 'coloureds', and then slaves, asserted their natural rights to freedom and equality. The Haitian Revolution broke out in 1791 and fighting continued until 1804 (independence) and beyond, during which time the economy and landscape were destroyed. Before the revolution sugar production in St Domingue was more than that of all the British islands combined, but production and exports quickly plummeted. Toussaint Louverture, an ex-slave himself, coordinated the fight for freedom of the enslaved. Bryan Edwards, a Jamaican merchant-planter, visited Haiti during the Revolution, graphically recording the deaths and destruction of sugar plantations and coffee estates.[8] Thousands of whites and loyal slaves were massacred before Haitian slaves won freedom. The Revolutionary French government, headed by the Jacobins, declared slaves free in all the French islands in 1794. Only Haitian slaves retained freedom because slavery was re-imposed in Martinique and Guadeloupe by Napoleon Bonaparte. Many Haitian whites fled to Cuba, Puerto Rico and Jamaica, taking their sugar and coffee expertise with them. Haitian exiles also landed in the United States, especially in Baltimore and Louisiana.

The Haitian Revolution had important repercussions in the wider Caribbean and elsewhere. News of events in Haiti spread and encouraged slave uprisings in other islands, such as Curaçao (1795) and Cuba (the Aponte Rebellion of 1812). Economically, Haitian exports of sugar and coffee stopped, driving up world prices. Planters in neighbouring islands, such as Jamaica, expanded production to increase profits. Because of a demand for labour, the slave trade rose to its height in the 1790s, even though abolitionists predicted dire consequences, using the spectre of Haiti as a warning. But, as David Brion Davis concluded, greed overcame fear.[9]

On the international scene, Spain, Britain and France all fought to gain control of St Domingue from the rebellious slaves, but all failed, with the loss of many men from battle wounds and diseases such as yellow fever. Haiti became independent from France in 1804 – becoming only the second republic (this one a black republic) in the Americas after the United States. The Amerindian name Haiti, meaning land of mountains, was chosen for the new country to reflect the rupture with Europe. A new Haitian emperor, Jean-Jacques Dessalines, was crowned, but assassinated two years later. Fighting continued between rival factions, and sections of society were militarized. Henri Christophe (who corresponded with William Wilberforce) became emperor in 1811, and ruled northern Haiti. Alexandre Pétion, a mulatto leader, ruled in the southern part of the country, before Jean-Pierre Boyer reunited Haiti in 1820. Haiti went on to dominate the western part of Hispaniola until the Dominican Republic broke free in 1844. In order to gain French recognition Haiti agreed to pay an indemnity of millions of francs, a heavy burden for a new republic. Unfortunately, the political instability and economic fragility of the early years have continued in Haiti to the present time.

THE NINETEENTH CENTURY

At the close of the Napoleonic Wars in 1815, the French empire in the Americas was reduced to Martinique and Guadeloupe. Haiti was lost to independence, and the Louisiana Territory was sold to the US in 1803 for $15 million to help pay for Napoleon's European wars. Later, Haiti invaded Santo Domingo. British Caribbean colonies increased when Trinidad, with extensive fertile land, was acquired from Spain. The Spanish empire, thrown into shock by Napoleon's occupation of Spain, moved towards independence. Revolutionary leaders, such as Simón Bolívar of Venezuela and José de San Martín of Argentina, organized armed resistance against Spanish rule. The Battle of Ayacucho, high in the Andes (1824), marked the defeat of Spain. By 1825 all the Spanish colonies on the mainland of Middle and South America were independent. Only Cuba and Puerto Rico remained within the Spanish American empire.

The nineteenth century brought big changes to the Caribbean region, the most significant being the end of slavery and the slave trade. Denmark outlawed the trade in slaves in 1802, the British ban came in 1807, and the Royal Navy tried to suppress the trade, with some success. One well-known historian has labelled the end of the British slave trade 'econocide', because he maintains that the slave trade and sugar complex were still profitable.[10] The United States banned the Atlantic slave trade in 1808, followed by the Netherlands in 1814. France outlawed the trade in 1831, and Spain did in 1845. The demand for slave labour in Cuba and Puerto Rico remained high for their expanding sugar industries.

Beginning in the 1830s the institution of slavery was phased out in the British colonies. Abolitionists, such as William Wilberforce and Thomas Fowell Buxton, both Members of Parliament, promoted legislation to end slavery in the British Empire. Slave rebellions in Barbados (1816) and Jamaica (1831) drove home the point that slaves would fight for freedom. Mass support in Britain (including strong backing from women), and changing economic and political realities, helped the case for emancipation. In 1833 the British parliament passed the Emancipation Act that included monetary compensation for planters (£20 million) and a period of apprenticeship for ex-slaves. 'Full Freedom' came in 1838.

After slave emancipation the production of sugar declined in some islands, notably Jamaica, where many ex-slaves established villages and worked agricultural plots away from plantations. On other islands, such as Barbados, sugar continued to be significant. Sugar production in the British colonies suffered a further blow when protection ended and free trade was introduced in the 1840s. In the British Caribbean long-established producers found it difficult to compete with large modern plantations opening in Cuba, which still had slaves until 1886. Additional competition came from sugar beet.

There has been much debate about the reasons behind the abolition of slavery in the British case. Was abolition motivated from humanitarian or economic motives? The answer is that both considerations played a role. Evangelicals mobilized popular support for emancipation, holding meetings up and down Britain. West Indian planters were losing political and economic clout in the face of increasing industrialization, a changing economy and demands for freer trade. Factory owners wanted cheaper food for the factory work force. Slavery looked more and more out of tune with emerging middle-class 'civilized' values. Slavery was no longer needed.

The French abolished slavery again in the revolutionary year of 1848, and the Dutch followed in 1863. Slaves in the Danish Virgin Islands rose up and won freedom in 1848. The last country to abolish slavery was Brazil in 1888. The end of slavery in the British, French and Dutch islands led to economic stagnation, economic decline and the growth of a free peasantry. It meant a shortage of plantation labour in some islands, such as Jamaica, as many ex-slaves (especially women) withdrew their labour from arduous sugar-cane work. The labour shortage led to an indentured labour scheme from the Indian subcontinent and China. Between 1838 and 1918 nearly 150,000 indentured workers moved from India to Trinidad. In a shorter period, 1853 to 1885, about 80,000 East Indians went to the French Caribbean. The ethnic mix of the region was enriched, but resentment followed. In Trinidad today there is still animosity between people of African and Indian heritage. Support for the two major political parties is divided along ethnic lines.

If slavery was on the decline in the islands controlled by North Europeans, the Spanish colonies of Puerto Rico and Cuba saw an increase in sugar plantation agriculture and slavery in the nineteenth century, as land was taken into cultivation, sugar plantations established, and slaves and indentured labourers imported. Cuba became the world's most important sugar producer, using new technologies (such as steam power), abundant fertile land, slave labour and US investment and tariff concessions. Between 1848 and 1874 approximately 125,000 Chinese indentured workers went to Cuba. By the 1850s Cuba was producing a large percentage of the world's sugar, and profits helped reduce Spain's trade deficit.

During the nineteenth century the United States' interest in the Caribbean increased. Beginning in 1823 with the Monroe Doctrine, the US tried to limit European penetration of the Americas. The US was setting the stage for dominance in the western hemisphere. In the years around mid-century, elements in the US, influenced by ideas of expansion and 'Manifest Destiny', talked about adding Cuba to the United States as a slave state. In 1848 President Polk suggested buying Cuba, and in 1854 President Franklin Pierce offered Spain over $100 million for the island. The Civil War turned US attention away from the Caribbean, although in 1868 President Ulysses S. Grant was in favour of annexing the Dominican Republic. Previously, between 1861 and 1865, the Dominican Republic, fearing Haitian dominance, was voluntarily accepted back into the Spanish empire.

After the Civil War US interests in the Greater Antilles centred on commercial and economic concerns – on sugar and tobacco rather than formal annexation. Cuban sugar production was the most advanced, with steam-powered mills and a rail network. By the 1870s the US was the major market for sugar from the Dominican Republic, Cuba and Puerto Rico. Its merchants shipped sugar and US companies refined, packaged and marketed it.

Slavery ended in Puerto Rico between 1873 and 1876 and in Cuba between 1880 and 1886. In Cuba the latter part of the nineteenth century was dominated by the struggle for independence from Spain, first with an unsuccessful Ten Years War between 1868 and 1878 that pitted Spanish troops against Cuban insurgents. The economy was disrupted and thousands died. Cubans wanted more autonomy and fewer restrictions on trade, especially with the United States. The successful war for Cuban independence was fought between 1895 and 1898. The Cuban patriots, led by José Martí (1853–1895) before his early death in the action, wanted full independence. Martí, a journalist and poet, had been banished to New York for revolutionary activities. He became the martyr of Cuban independence. The three years of war cost an estimated 400,000 lives, and featured cruel treatment by Spanish soldiers.[11] Sugar production declined as many plantations were torched. During the fighting Spain granted Puerto Rico internal self-government in 1897, shortly before US annexation.

In 1898 the United States got involved in the Spanish-American War, after the US warship *Maine* exploded in Havana harbour in February in mysterious circumstances, giving the US a cause for war. Hostilities were brief. Peace was signed in Paris in December 1898. In addition to Puerto Rico, the US gained the Philippines and Guam, Spanish colonies in the Pacific. Cuba was occupied. The US became an imperial power in the Caribbean, displacing Spain. By the Platt Amendment of 1901, Cuba became in effect a US protectorate, with the US assuming the right to intervene in Cuban affairs. In 1903 the United States leased the naval base at Guantánamo Bay under a treaty that can only be revoked by mutual Cuban–US agreement. At the height of the Age of Imperialism, when expanding European empires were being carved out in Africa and Asia, the United States, fearing additional European penetration in the region, and wanting overseas bases, issued the Roosevelt Corollary to the Monroe Doctrine (1904), and assumed the right to intervene directly in Caribbean affairs. The Corollary was withdrawn in 1934, although the US has since intervened many times.

WORLD WAR I AND THE GREAT DEPRESSION

The strategic significance of the Caribbean to the United States was reinforced by the construction of the Panama Canal, which opened in 1914, just in time for World War I. The Panama Canal, built and controlled by the US government (after a failed French attempt), linked the Atlantic and the Pacific, and cut thousands of miles off the voyage from the east to the west coast of the US. Just as the Suez Canal was considered crucial to British global and imperial interests, the Panama

Canal was vital to the United States for economic and military reasons. The construction of the canal demonstrated the technological power of the United States. It was also testimony to the work of Caribbean people – men from Jamaica, Barbados and other islands – who provided most of the labour. Many died from diseases, such as yellow fever, and from accidents. Some went home with 'Panama money'; some stayed in Central America, where they form significant populations in coastal communities.

Cuba, the Dominican Republic and Haiti

The building of the Panama Canal increased US concern about the security of the Caribbean region. US marines were in Cuba between 1906 and 1909 and again between 1917 and 1922 due to political and economic crises. The US occupied Haiti in 1915 and the Dominican Republic the following year, partly due to World War I (1914–18) and security reasons, partly for financial and commercial reasons. The US did not want European countries intervening in Haiti or the Dominican Republic to collect debts. Fearing German penetration in the region, the US purchased the Virgin Islands from Denmark in 1917, the same year that Puerto Ricans became US citizens. In 1932 residents of the US Virgin Islands became US citizens.

Hispanic areas in the Greater Antilles were coming more and more under US influence and control, as they relied on capital, credit, markets and companies in North America. US economic dominance in the Greater Antilles revolved around the expansion of sugar cane plantations and the manufacture of sugar. During World War I the US contracted to buy large amounts of Cuban sugar and, with sugar prices high, American interests bought up land and sugar mills. As commercial plantations expanded many Cuban peasants lost land and became wage labourers dependent on foreign firms. Similar developments occurred in the Dominican Republic and Puerto Rico. 'The overwhelming presence of US sugar interests in the Greater Antilles in the early twentieth century led . . . to a massive takeover of peoples and lands . . .'.[12] Economic control was in the hands of the US.

In addition, the US Navy was paramount in the region, as the British West India squadron was reduced. US troops and civilian personnel remained in the Dominican Republic until 1924, and in Haiti until 1934 and Franklin D. Roosevelt's 'Good Neighbor Policy'. Even after departure the US retained the right to oversee customs affairs in both countries. During US occupation attempts were made to reorganize finances, cut corruption and establish stability. Local infrastructure, such as roads, power, and water supplies, were improved. Schools and hospitals were built. But little was achieved in relation to democratic government and responsibility. Racism was rampant. One criticism levelled at the Americans is that, as part of an exit strategy, they trained brutal armed police forces in the Dominican Republic and Haiti. Some commentators suggest that the US legacy helped to set the stage for dictators like Rafael Trujillo in the Dominican Republic, Fulgencio Batista in Cuba and the Duvaliers ('Papa Doc' and 'Baby Doc') in Haiti, who used police forces for repression and to sustain power.[13]

US intervention and occupation in the region met with local resistance. In the Dominican Republic, for example, opposition came from peasants who had lost land to expanding sugar companies. One famous Dominican rebel leader was General Ramón Natera. In Haiti rebels typically ambushed marines and then disappeared into the countryside, where they drew support from peasant villages. In Haiti the US tried to revive the corvée, or forced labour system, to help with road-building projects, resulting in an uprising led by Charlemagne Peralte. He became a hero and martyr when killed by US marines. In Puerto Rico nationalist sentiment (symbolized by the local peasant figure of the *jibaro*) and anti-American feeling formed a platform for the creation of the Popular Democratic Party in 1938 led by Luis Muñoz Marín. He gathered widespread support and won the election of 1940.

If US military intervention led to political repercussions, the impact of the Great Depression (which began in the US with the Wall Street Crash of 1929) reverberated throughout the Caribbean, bringing widespread economic hardship and poverty. Cuba was especially hard hit. Sugar production and prices fell drastically. Sugar exports more than halved between 1928 and 1933. Wages were cut; unemployment rose;

student protests and worker strikes were organized. By 1933 the Cuban president, General Gerardo Machado, faced revolutionary chaos, involving violence and bombings. Machado resigned, and after further strikes and violence, Fulgencio Batista, an army sergeant, emerged as the most powerful man in Cuba, elected president in 1940.

Puerto Rico also suffered throughout the Depression years. Sugar, tobacco and the needlework industries were all badly affected. Unemployment and destitution were common. Many blamed dependence on the United States for economic woes.

In the Dominican Republic General Rafael Trujillo ruled as a dictator from 1930 until assassinated in 1961. In common with other authoritarian rulers of the time, such as Benito Mussolini in Italy, he was ruthless and repressive (using a secret police), but undertook internal improvements and agricultural development. The sugar industry grew with North American investment. Rice and maize crops increased significantly on government-sponsored agricultural colonies. After the capital of Santo Domingo was hit by a hurricane in 1930 (killing several thousand people), Trujillo spent liberally on rebuilding the city with modern suburbs, an art gallery and a museum to promote national pride. The capital was renamed Trujillo, before reverting to Santo Domingo in 1961 with the demise of the dictator. The Dominican Republic was modernized, but at the price of freedom.

A most famous act of brutality came in 1937 when Haitian migrants/squatters (possibly over 10,000) were murdered in the border region between the Dominican Republic and Haiti on Trujillo's orders. This incident is still bitterly remembered. Border issues continue to plague relations between these neighbours since Haitians frequently seek work in the more prosperous Dominican Republic.

British, French and Dutch colonies

During the first half of the twentieth century, British, French and Dutch colonial control continued in the Lesser Antilles and Jamaica. Troops from the Anglo-Caribbean islands fought and died in World War I, and were politicized by their experiences abroad. The war was a catalyst for political reform. The British West Indies Regiment included over 15,000 volunteers from across the Anglo-Caribbean, of whom over 1,000 lost their lives in the Great War. Between 1917 and 1919 there were riots and strikes in Jamaica, Trinidad and elsewhere. Middle-class organizations, including women's groups, began to push for political change and social reform.

During and after the war Marcus Garvey (1887–1940) became a prominent black leader, advocating equal rights, black nationalism and economic independence. He left Jamaica and set up a branch of his Universal Negro Improvement Association (UNIA) in New York in 1916. His organization soon opened across the Caribbean and attracted wide membership, not just in the Anglo-Caribbean islands but elsewhere, such as in Cuba. Garvey was a dynamic speaker who preached black pride, a back-to-Africa movement and pan-Africanism. He started a newspaper, *Negro World*, in New York in 1917, and founded the Black Star steamship company. In 1923 he was convicted of using the US postal service to defraud, spending three years in jail before being deported to Jamaica. Garvey, politically active in Jamaica between 1928 and 1935, was an inspiration to many in the Caribbean who were tired of racism, discrimination and exploitation.

Politically, the British islands were controlled by local white elites and British Government officials. Islands, with the exception of Barbados and the Bahamas, were under 'Crown Colony' government, where members of the executive branch (the governor and senior officials) were appointed by politicians in Westminster. After World War I demands for reform resulted in the Colonial Office sending E.F.L. Wood (later Lord Halifax, Foreign Secretary and Ambassador to Washington) to the Caribbean in 1921. On Wood's advice, elected members were added to Legislative Councils in Trinidad and Tobago, and other islands.[14] The franchise was restricted by property qualifications. Majority black rule came after World War II. The French colonies had representation in the Paris National Assembly, a system that would later evolve into the concept of overseas *départements*.

Tropical agriculture continued to be the dominant economic activity in many islands, although in the early years of the twentieth century the petroleum industry in Trinidad, and oil refining in Curaçao and Aruba (using Venezuelan crude oil), developed. As a consequence the industrial labour force grew, unions developed and demands were made for higher wages and better living conditions. Unions turned economic pressure into political action. The Trinidad Workingmen's Association, formed in 1919 by returning World War I veterans and dockworkers, became the Trinidad Labour Party in 1934.

The Depression years of the 1930s saw widespread labour unrest in the Caribbean as sugar prices dropped, wages fell, people lost jobs and migrant workers returned home due to unemployment elsewhere, such as Cuba and the Dominican Republic. Health, education and housing were abysmal, malnutrition common. In 1931 the infant mortality rate in Jamaica was 154, and in Barbados a staggering 298, per 1,000 live births.[15] Caribbean economies were in dire straits, and violence erupted. In St Kitts sugar workers went on strike for higher wages and better conditions in 1935. The same happened in St Vincent. In St Lucia coal loaders at Castries went on strike, and in 1937 oil workers in Trinidad. A labour leader, Uriah 'Buzz' Butler, was arrested, and some protesters were shot. Rioting occurred in Bridgetown, Barbados, after the deportation of Clement Payne, a union organizer from Trinidad. The police shot and wounded several Barbadians. Similarly, in Jamaica, economic discontent boiled over into strikes and violence, and Jamaicans were killed. Trade unions pushed for better conditions and the right to collective bargaining. Local leaders emerged – Norman Manley and Alexander Bustamante in Jamaica, Uriah Butler and Eric Williams in Trinidad, Grantley Adams in Barbados and Robert Bradshaw in St Kitts. The development of political parties and unions went hand in hand. Aspiring politicians wanted universal suffrage and better living standards for the black population.

The British Government responded to the violence of the 1930s with the famous Moyne Commission (1938) to study economic and social issues in the West Indies. It revealed alarming conditions. The Commission recommended the expansion of social services and the welfare state to ease economic suffering and quell unrest, and showed the need for increased investment in colonial development programmes. The Commission's findings (not fully published until 1945) partly inspired the Colonial Welfare and Development Act of

1940, which later helped with housing and education. In Jamaica, constitutional reforms followed in 1944, permitting universal suffrage over the age of 21 and more internal self-government.

WORLD WAR II (1939–45)

World War II had a big impact on the Caribbean region. Demand for raw materials, especially bauxite, nickel and petroleum (but also sugar), increased, as nations mobilized for war. Prices were good for some commodities, and jobs increased after the terrible Depression years. Sugar exports to Britain and Canada were guaranteed and prices rose. Some exports, notably bananas and cigars, ceased because of lack of cargo space.

In the early phase of World War II the colonial powers of France and the Netherlands were defeated by Germany (June 1940). What would happen to the French and Dutch colonies? Would they fall under German control? Britain was busy trying to prevent invasion by Germany and had little capacity to defend its Caribbean colonies, or prevent German penetration of the region. The United States and others signed the Act of Havana in July 1940 in an attempt to safeguard the islands. In essence it was a re-statement of the Monroe Doctrine, saying that territories in the western hemisphere could not be transferred to other powers. Canadian troops were moved into the Caribbean to strengthen forces there. Even before the US joined the Allied side against Germany in December 1941 (after the Japanese attack on Pearl Harbor), it was clear where US sympathies lay. At the height of the Battle of Britain in September 1940 Franklin D. Roosevelt transferred 50 destroyers to Britain in return for bases in Newfoundland, Bermuda, the Bahamas, Jamaica, Antigua, Trinidad and British Guyana. The outcome was that the islands became more dependent on the United States, but none of the islands fell under German rule, although German U-boats were active in the Caribbean, sinking hundreds of ships. The Netherlands Antilles fared well in the war with the high demand for oil and the transfer of some Dutch corporate assets to the islands, especially Curaçao. Because Martinique and Guadeloupe were under Vichy rule, an Allied blockade led to hardship.

A further impact of World War II, and of Caribbean peoples' participation in the war effort, was political liberalization, although initially activists, such as Butler of Trinidad, were interned. Thousands of Anglo-Caribbean troops risked their lives for the empire, and hastened the movement to democracy. Universal adult suffrage was achieved in Jamaica in 1944, Trinidad in 1945, Barbados in 1950 and other islands in 1951. Elected majorities in legislative councils came in the 1950s. Britain was exhausted by the war. The road to independence lay ahead.

Chapter 3

Caribbean Foreign Relations since 1945

BACKGROUND

As US power grew in the twentieth century, colonial control from outside the Caribbean region diminished. In 1898 Spain ceded Puerto Rico to the United States. Shortly afterwards the base at Guantánamo Bay was acquired as Cuba became a US protectorate. The US built the Panama Canal and, in the view of Admiral Mahan, the famous American naval strategist, the canal (completed in 1914) transformed the Caribbean from a terminus into a major sea route linking the Atlantic and the Pacific oceans. By 1910 Britain had removed major Royal Navy units from the Caribbean, confident that the US had the naval capability to secure the seaways. In 1917 the US bought the Danish Caribbean islands to create the US Virgin Islands.

In World War II US military presence increased. In Puerto Rico the Roosevelt Roads naval station and a new airforce base were completed. The US Virgin Islands got a submarine base and airfields.[1] Bases were built, with British consent, at Bermuda, the Bahamas, Jamaica, Antigua, St Lucia, Trinidad and on the South American mainland at Guyana. Britain received 50 destroyers in return. The United States considers the Caribbean essential for security and protection, and has consistently intervened in the region. Against this background the islands try to maintain a sense of independence and integrity.

The islands are important to the US for a number of reasons. Strategically, the Caribbean islands lie on major trade routes from Europe, the Middle East and Africa to the east coast of North America, the Gulf of Mexico and the approaches to the Panama Canal. Petroleum supplies and other strategic goods are shipped through Caribbean waters, and significant amounts of oil are refined in the area. In terms of location the islands are close to the US, with Cuba only 90 miles away from Florida. Just as Britain was historically concerned to ensure that Ireland did not become a base for potential enemies, so the US has tried to keep Caribbean islands out of enemy hands. That is why Cuban links with the Soviet Union were so controversial.

Another reason for US interest in the region is that migrants are a significant Caribbean export and many people of Caribbean heritage live in the US. Some are legal immigrants; others are undocumented. For example, the Miami area is home to over a million Cuban exiles, many of whom actively oppose normalizing relations with Castro. The numbers of undocumented Cubans attempting to reach the US varies according to economic conditions on the island. In 2005 over 2,500 arrived on the Florida shore. Under the 'dry foot' policy they were allowed to stay in the US. About 2,800 Cubans were apprehended at sea, and, as 'wet foot' migrants, were sent home. Each year 20,000 Cubans can move legally to the United States, thanks to an agreement of 1994, but many more attempt the journey, either across the sea or via Mexico. New York has a concentration of Puerto Ricans, who, as US citizens, come and go as they please. Many other Caribbean migrants enter the US via Puerto Rico. New York is a magnet for people from the Dominican Republic and Haiti, and many migrants from the English-speaking Caribbean make their home in the northeast United States. Some of the internationally famous people with Caribbean roots include political activist Marcus Garvey (Jamaica), politician Shirley Chisholm (from Barbados), Malcolm X (mother from Grenada), US Secretary of State Colin Powell (parents from Jamaica), Oscar de la Renta (New York fashion designer from the Dominican Republic) and actress/singer Jennifer Lopez (Puerto Rico). Many migrants have a transnational identity and operate in various cultural settings.

Lastly, the Caribbean attracts US attention because of illegal activities, including drug running and money laundering. The Caribbean is in effect the 'third border' of the United States, where surveillance is enforced, and intervention, both overt and covert, is expected.

IMPACT OF WORLD WAR II

After World War II the unlikely alliance of the United States and the Soviet Union, formed in response to German and Japanese aggression, quickly evaporated. The outcome was the Cold War – an ideological conflict that did not ignite into a major hot war, but saw many proxy fights around the globe. Communism faced capitalism as the 'iron curtain' came down in Central Europe. The Soviets gained control of Eastern Europe (including East Germany), and tried to promote communism around the world. The Truman Doctrine (1947) outlined the US commitment to support democracy and contain communism. The United States assisted the reconstruction of Western Europe via the Marshall Plan, and resisted the spread of communism, first in Europe, then in Korea and Vietnam. The North Atlantic Treaty Organization (NATO), a military alliance between America, Canada and most of Western Europe, was established in 1949 for protection against the expansion of the Soviet Union and its satellites.

The Organization of American States (OAS) dates from 1890 but in 1948 it adopted a formal charter to encourage inter-American cooperation and settle disputes. It includes 32 member nations from Latin America and the Caribbean. Cuba, an original member, has been excluded since 1962. In 1954, in the heat of the Cold War, the OAS adopted the 'Caracas Declaration', announcing that international communism was incompatible with democratic freedoms in the Americas. Most members agreed with the resolution. But Mexico and Argentina abstained, and Guatemala opposed the motion.

What of the Caribbean in the Cold War era? After World War II the US, nervous about 'creeping communism', supported right-wing governments in the region, including the repressive regimes of Rafael Trujillo in the Dominican Republic (1930–61), 'Papa Doc' (1957–71) and 'Baby Doc' (1971–86) Duvalier in Haiti, and Fulgencio Batista in Cuba (president 1940–44 and dictator 1952–9). Right-wing dictatorships seemed preferable to communists. As we shall see, the Caribbean became a major site for confrontation between the US and the Soviets after Castro took power in Cuba in 1959.

A major consequence of World War II was that European colonial powers – Britain, France and the Netherlands – were all weakened by the conflict. Demands for political liberalization and de-colonization were in the air, and, because of strained economic circumstances, the Europeans responded. Even before the war's end, Caribbean people in the British islands were demanding more voice in politics, and after the war there was gradual movement towards representative government, with extension of the suffrage and local control of internal affairs, before full independence.

In 1946 Martinique and Guadeloupe became overseas departments (*départements d'outre-mer*) of France with full representation in the National Assembly and Senate in Paris, in addition to elected island councils. Suspicious of US intentions and expansion, the French were in favour of assimilating their Caribbean colonies. And, in 1954, the Netherlands Antilles were recognized as autonomous, equal parts of the Kingdom of the Netherlands, with control over internal affairs.

Meanwhile, in Puerto Rico, the US promoted 'Operation Bootstrap' – a programme of economic and industrial development launched in 1947. Luis Muñoz Marín, the first elected Governor of Puerto Rico (1948), favoured industrialization, realizing that the island could capitalize on low wages and low taxes. The agricultural economy of coffee, sugar and tobacco would not support higher living standards. Marín, of the Popular Democratic Party, was successful and won re-election until leaving office in 1964. In 1952 Puerto Rico gained 'commonwealth' status with the US as a free associated state (*estado libre asociado*), which translated into internal self-government, with defence, customs and foreign policy in US hands.

During the 1950s Cuba was in crisis involving social and economic grievances and discontent with the corrupt dictatorship of Fulgencio Batista (1901–1973), who had seized power in a 1952 military coup. Inflation and unemployment were high. Wealth was concentrated in the hands of a few. Rural poverty and urban penury were pervasive. The economy relied on sugar exports, and failed to diversify, although American tourists and celebrities visited Cuba. Gambling and prostitution thrived. US interests were intrusive, and became targets for nationalist sentiment. Foreign control of the economy was resented.[2] Cuba would become a focal point for Cold War confrontation between the United States and the Soviet Union in the western hemisphere.

Fidel Castro, educated as a lawyer, and the illegitimate son of a landowning sugar planter who had migrated from Spain to fight in the Spanish-American War, challenged the Batista regime by leading an attack on the Moncado barracks in Santiago de Cuba on 26 July 1953. The attack failed miserably. Castro served two years (of a fifteen-year sentence) in prison, before being given amnesty and going into exile, mostly in Mexico. There he planned revolutionary action with Ernesto 'Che' Guevara, originally from Argentina. In 1956 Castro returned to Cuba on the *Granma* with about 80 followers. Nearly all were killed by Batista's forces on arrival, but the survivors began guerrilla operations in the Sierra Maestra Mountains, in the south-east of Cuba. Castro's activities and other insurgency culminated in a successful, popular insurrection against the regime in 1959. Batista fled to the Dominican Republic and Castro took over the government, at first with tacit US approval.

Inside Cuba there was pressure for radical change from supporters of the revolution – the urban proletariat, rural peasants and the unemployed and under-employed – who made up a majority of the population. Expectations for social and economic justice mounted. The revolutionary government, with Castro as prime minister, re-negotiated labour contracts and raised wages, notably of cane farmers. Health and education reforms were planned. Legal discrimination against blacks was abolished. Rents on houses were cut and so were electric and telephone rates. The Agrarian Reform Law of May 1959 nationalized large landholdings (including the Castro family farm) and created co-operatives and state farms. Nationalization affected the great landowners, and US-owned sugar companies, who held a large percentage of arable land. Compensation was proposed, but in the form of twenty-year Cuban bonds. Some businesses, notably the Bacardi rum operation, were taken over by the government. The Bacardis continued production in Puerto Rico. Officials in the US expressed frustration, and warned that sugar quota exports to the US might be curtailed. The US reaction encouraged Castro to look to the Soviets, who offered a guaranteed market for sugar, as well as cheap Soviet petroleum. In February 1960 Castro made a deal with the Soviets that would have them buy 5 million tons of Cuban sugar. Castro moved closer to the Soviet camp, and also relied more and more on the Cuban Communist Party for support and personnel. In common with many dictators, he liquidated or imprisoned political opponents and many former supporters who had worked with him against Batista.

In 1960 the Cuban government told American-owned oil companies, such as Standard Oil and Texaco, to refine petroleum from cheaper Soviet sources. When the companies refused, the Cuban government nationalized the refineries. The US retaliated by eliminating the sugar quota. Castro responded by nationalizing additional US companies and resources, including utilities, sugar mills, banks and hotels, this time without compensation. The US banned exports to Cuba, excepting food and medicine. In 1961 the United States cut diplomatic relations with Cuba, a country now tied increasingly to the Soviet bloc.

Events in Cuba brought the Cold War to the western hemisphere and into the Caribbean basin. The US tried to isolate Cuba, at first diplomatically. Then a military solution was devised. The CIA (established in 1947) planned a 'covert operation' to remove Castro, using a group of about 1,500 Miami Cuban exiles. On 17 April 1961 the force, expecting a sympathetic Cuban uprising, landed at the Bay of Pigs on the south coast of Cuba. No local support was forthcoming; the US withheld promised air support; and the episode was a disaster. Within a few days most invaders were either killed or captured. More than 1,000 were tried and imprisoned, but later exchanged for US food and medicine valued at over $50 million. The US looked incompetent and Castro's stock rose inside Cuba and in anti-US international circles.

Cuba moved even closer to the Soviets. There were no free elections and no free press. Remaining opposition groups were imprisoned and many Cubans left the island for Florida. It is telling that over half the faculty of the University of Havana found it advisable to leave Cuba, many settling in the United States.[3] Between 1960 and 1962 over 60,000 Cubans, mostly middle-class professionals and technicians, left each year. The revolution was solidified by the emigration of opponents, who initially believed their exile would be short. Some commentators believe the Cuban revolution evolved into a socialist revolution. Louis A. Pérez, an authority on Cuban history, maintains there was no initial plan to go the socialist route; instead it was 'more improvised than calculated, more reaction than intention'.[4] Others, perhaps including Castro himself, would say he was a Marxist all along. In December 1961, Castro declared himself a Marxist-Leninist.

Relations between Cuba and the United States deteriorated further as the US-imposed trade embargo began to hurt. The US encouraged other countries to follow suit. The Organization of American States supported the embargo between 1964 and 1975. Industry and manufacturing in Cuba suffered because Cuba relied on US companies for replacement parts for industrial infrastructure and transportation systems. Then, in the autumn of 1962, aerial photos made it clear that the USSR was supplying arms to Cuba and installing ballistic missile sites. The US government, headed by President John F. Kennedy, was aware that Soviet ships were heading to Cuba with offensive weapons (possibly atomic warheads). In response, the US Navy blockaded Cuba, and the Russians, under President Krushchev, were told to remove the missile sites that threatened US cities. Nuclear war was imminent. Commentators agree that this was the closest the world has come to nuclear conflagration. In the end a compromise was reached. The Soviets stopped work on Cuban missile sites; the US lifted the blockade and promised not to invade Cuba. NATO missiles, which threatened the Soviet Union, were quietly removed from Turkey. Castro resented not being fully engaged in negotiations with Russia and the US, but the realities of superpower politics were made clear. In retaliation, he flirted with Marxist China for a while, but Russia remained the major trade partner and benefactor.

In 1961 the Kennedy administration had initiated the 'Alliance for Progress' to stimulate economic development in the Caribbean and Latin America, and isolate Castro. The Punta del Este conference in Uruguay, which launched the Alliance, was attended by representatives of all American countries except Cuba. The United States, acting in response to a perceived threat, tried to win support with economic assistance and incentives. The Alliance for Progress was designed as a ten-year plan to support economic development, raise per capita income, promote agricultural reform and improve education, housing and health care, while fostering the growth of democracy. The United States contributed over $10 billion from its Agency of International Development, but much of the aid went to support old regimes rather than generate reform.

During the 1960s and '70s Russia provided Cuba with trade and aid. Cuban sugar was purchased by the Soviets above world prices, and Soviet oil was traded to Cuba at favourable rates. In 1969 Castro mobilized the nation for the 'ten-million-ton sugar harvest', which diverted manpower and resources to the effort. The goal was not achieved. The Soviets still supported Cuban economic development with technical assistance and industrial modernization. Cuba ran up a huge debt with their communist sponsors. The US attempted to destabilize Cuba, not least with several CIA plots to assassinate Castro, which served only to promote Cuban nationalism. In the 1970s the Cuban Communist Party increasingly exercised power, and party membership grew.[5]

As elsewhere in the Cold War, US efforts in the Caribbean focused on preventing the spread of communism. In 1960 'Papa Doc' Duvalier, autocratic president of Haiti, a former medical doctor and promoter of Haiti's African heritage, played on US fears by feigning interest in Soviet aid. He was rewarded with US funds for a new airport.[6] Nervous about developments that smacked of left-wing politics, and anxious to stop a 'second Cuba' in the region, the US intervened in the Dominican Republic in 1965. The situation was complicated because in 1963 Juan Bosch, the elected president of the country and leader of the Dominican Revolutionary Party, had been ousted by the military and conservative elites, who feared his socialist leanings. In 1965 supporters of Bosch rallied to restore him to power and the Dominican Republic erupted in violence. President Lyndon Johnson sent over 20,000 marines to restore order. An inter-American force, voted for by the OAS, was later deployed. After a corrupt election, where Bosch supporters were intimidated or worse, Joaquín Balaguer, a right-wing former Trujillo supporter, was elected president in 1966, which satisfied the military and business sector of the Dominican Republic, and US interests. The Balaguer government received millions of dollars in aid from the US. The United States had shown again its willingness to intervene in the region, with military force if necessary.

Cuba developed an independent international policy in the 1960s and '70s, with the aim of becoming a leader in Third World politics. Cuban technicians, doctors, engineers and teachers helped with social and economic projects around the world. In Latin America the Cuban government supported guerrilla movements in Guatemala, Colombia, Venezuela, Peru and Bolivia. In Africa, during 1975–6, Cuba provided several thousand troops (with Russian tanks) to support the Popular Movement for the Liberation of Angola (MPLA) against the western-backed UNITA (National Union for the Total Independence of Angola). Cuban forces stayed in Angola until 1990. In 1978 Cuban troops were dispatched to Ethiopia to stop an invasion from Somalia.

Cuban visibility on the world scene reached its height in 1979 when Havana hosted the summit for the Nonaligned Movement, which included India. Fidel Castro, serving as chair of the conference, projected himself as a leader of the Third World, firmly opposed to imperialist oppression. A few months later, however, Cuba's ally and supporter, the Soviet Union, invaded Afghanistan, a poor Third World state. Because Cuba would not support a UN vote to condemn the Soviets, Cuba lost prestige among countries in the Nonaligned Movement.

Still, in the Americas, Cuba seemed to be acquiring allies. In July 1979 the Marxist-leaning *Sandinistas*, led by Daniel Ortega, gained control in Nicaragua, forcing out the dictator Anastasio Somoza. The same year, in Grenada, the left-wing New Jewel Movement, headed by Maurice Bishop, overthrew the elected government of Prime Minister Sir Eric Gairy (formerly a militant trade-union leader) and seized power. The US-backed Gairy government had become corrupt and repressive, using a militia, known as the 'Mongoose Gang', to threaten opponents. Maurice Bishop, a London-educated lawyer, wanted to improve social and economic conditions and cooperate with Cuba. In 1983 a more militant Marxist group, led by Bernard Coard, arrested, 'tried' and executed Bishop, taking control of Grenada, an island with a total population of 100,000. Cold War tensions mounted as Cuba began to build a base on Grenada. Urged by leaders in the Commonwealth Caribbean (notably Eugenia Charles, Prime Minister of Dominica), US President Ronald Reagan dispatched a task force to rid Grenada of the Marxists and restore democracy. Without consulting London (which caused resentment), the US sent troops under the pretence of safeguarding the lives of US medical students in Grenada. The United States would not tolerate another communist regime in the Caribbean, and feared that the airport Cuba was building at Point Salines would be used for military purposes. The incident illustrated that every Caribbean island, no matter how small, is strategically and militarily important to the United States. Grenada was the last Cold War battleground in the Caribbean.

The US followed up the Grenada invasion with a plan to promote economic development for friendly states in the region. The Caribbean Basin Initiative (CBI) began in 1984. It provided favourable loans and investments to certain Caribbean states, not including Cuba or Nicaragua. Garments assembled in the region were to pay only a value added tax on entry into the US market, and duty free status was extended to some products. The Dominican Republic and Jamaica benefited most, although total investment was disappointing.

DE-COLONIZATION AND INDEPENDENCE IN THE ANGLO-CARIBBEAN

World War II eroded European empires. In the two decades after World War II the number of people living within the British Empire decreased from 700 million to 5 million, of which 3 million were in Hong Kong.[7] The post-World War II mood was anti-colonial, especially in the United States. India and Pakistan were the first to gain independence in 1947–8, followed by de-colonization in the British Caribbean and the 'winds of change' in Africa. After the failure of the West Indies Federation (discussed in the next chapter), Jamaica and Trinidad and Tobago became independent in 1962. Barbados and Guyana followed in 1966. Many of the other islands became self-governing 'Associated States' with Britain, before graduating to full independence in the 1970s: the Bahamas in 1973, Grenada the next year, Dominica in 1978, St Lucia and St Vincent in 1979. Antigua and Barbuda and St Kitts-Nevis achieved independence in the early 1980s. Several small territories, including volcano-ravaged Montserrat, the Turks and Caicos Islands, the offshore-banking Cayman Islands, and the British Virgin Islands are United Kingdom Overseas Territories with full UK citizenship.

Independent Caribbean states tried to promote agendas on the world scene but found it difficult to do so in the polarized environment of the Cold War. The US, fearing the attraction of the Cuban model, took the view that 'if you are not with us, you are against us'. The spread of socialism, even democratic socialism, was feared and resented by the US, most notably in the case of Jamaica.

Independence in the British Caribbean was, for the most part, a peaceful and amicable development, part of an evolutionary process, not a revolutionary outburst. Caribbean people had sown the seeds of independence in the 1930s and '40s, when leaders such as Alexander Bustamente and Norman Manley of Jamaica and Grantley Adams and Errol Barrow of Barbados organized unions and political groups to push for change. Most newly independent countries of the Caribbean chose to become members of the Commonwealth – an organization of former British colonies that is currently composed of 54 states, including populous India, Pakistan and Nigeria, and includes about a third of the world's population. Ten members of the Commonwealth are in the Caribbean, including Jamaica, Trinidad and Tobago, Barbados, Bahamas, Grenada, Dominica, St Vincent, St Lucia, Antigua-Barbuda, and St Kitts-Nevis, together with the UK Overseas Territories. Most, with the exception of Trinidad and Tobago, recognize Queen Elizabeth II as head of state. Core principles of the Commonwealth include a belief in political democracy, human rights, good governance, the rule of law and protection of the environment by sustainable development. The Commonwealth also provides an economic development network. The Canadian Government and Canadian corporations have invested heavily in the Caribbean, and Canadian banks are well represented in the region.

British influence in the Caribbean has continued to decline as the role of the United States in the region has increased. As we have seen, this geopolitical fact was underlined in 1983 when the US invaded Grenada without first consulting the UK. Both France and the Netherlands have, in general, played subdued roles in the Caribbean since World War II, opting to transform colonies into full partners of the metropolitan body politic. Strong economic links, however, remain between centres in France and the Netherlands and their associated Caribbean islands. Financial aid makes the French- and Dutch-connected islands among the richest in the region.

POST COLD WAR

During the 1990s, as the Soviet Union disintegrated, Cuba faced enormous problems adjusting to the decline of Soviet support. The country lost supplies of cheap oil, machinery and fertilizers. In addition, a generous line of credit dried up. The Cuban government responded by approaching Spain, Canada, Mexico and China for trade links and investment. Cuba attracted tourists from Europe, Canada and Latin America. The US strengthened the economic embargo with passage of the Helms-Burton Act (1996), which attempted to penalize foreign companies dealing with Cuba. Other countries ignored US threats and continued to do business with Cuba. Castro survived.

Meanwhile, in the early 1990s Haiti was in turmoil when the elected president, Jean-Bertrand Aristide, a Roman Catholic priest, was ejected from power by a military takeover. Aristide had little political experience, and frightened the middle and upper classes (and the military leaders) with his incendiary appeals to the masses. With Haitians taking to boats en route for America, the United States (with UN knowledge) intervened to quell the turmoil. Aristide was returned to power in 1994. Despite attempts at democratic government, Haiti experienced economic and social problems, and corruption was rampant. In 1997 international aid was stopped because effective reform measures were not in place. More recently, the Bush administration 'persuaded' Aristide to leave Haiti after rioting and disturbances in 2004. The OAS currently has forces there (mainly from Brazil and Chile) attempting to keep the peace. The election of February 2006 promised hope of stability.

Since the terrorist attacks of 11 September 2001, the United States has been engaged in Afghanistan and Iraq, diverting attention from the western hemisphere. The Caribbean has been neglected. Yet the strategic significance of the region remains vital to US interests. Gary Elbow has identified four important security issues for US policy-makers in relation to the Caribbean:

Political stability in the region is important.
Access to resources, especially petroleum, refined and shipped through the region, is crucial to the US economy.
Migration from the area to the US needs to be monitored and controlled.
The flow of drugs from and through the Caribbean needs constant surveillance.[8]

Two countries – Haiti and Cuba – illustrate the importance of these issues to the United States. Haiti is politically unstable and economically miserable. These conditions encourage Haitian migration, and cause problems in the region, not least in the neighbouring Dominican Republic. Haitian migrants seek access to the US directly, and via Puerto Rico. Haitian poverty breeds political discontent and stimulates criminal activity in relation to drugs, gangs and possibly terrorist activity.

Cuba will pose problems for the US when Castro departs. The eventual transition to a new government in Cuba could lead to political turmoil. Would the US intervene or allow circumstances to take their own course? How will the Cuban exiles, their children and grandchildren in Miami react to the end of Castro's rule? How will they try to influence US policy? Certainly, when Castro departs, the exiles will press for regime change and not a continuation of Marxist rule. However, regime change might produce economic chaos, as dispossessed property owners mount lawsuits to gain compensation and restitution.

Are there challengers to US hegemony in the region? President Hugo Chávez of Venezuela has ambitions to be a leader in Latin America. Venezuela has a history of economic links with the Netherlands ABC islands based on petroleum. Venezuela has a border dispute with its neighbour, Guyana, formerly a British colony. President Chávez has been vocally opposed to the Bush government and US free trade policies, most recently at the United Nations General Assembly in 2006, where he gained support in some Latin American circles for his anti-American stance. He uses petroleum to make friends and influence policy in the region, providing low-cost oil to Cuba and other Caribbean countries. Chávez recently gained publicity by offering cut-rate petroleum to New York and Massachusetts for low-income residents. That did not sit well with the Bush administration, but was favourably received in the north-east United States. Castro has an ally in Venezuela and together the two *caudillos* could be a focal point for forces opposed to 'Yankee' power. In Bolivia, the socialist leader Evo Morales was recently elected president. He counts Castro and Chávez as allies, and has verbally stood up to US power. A coca farmer himself, he promised to end a US-backed campaign to eradicate coca fields. Coca is the raw material for cocaine. Morales promises to keep Bolivian assets, including natural gas, in Bolivian hands.

Is there potential for Chinese influence in the region? China's economy is growing rapidly and needs raw materials such as food and metals (like nickel from Cuba) to sustain economic growth. China now buys more copper from Chile than the US does, and Chinese demand for materials is driving up commodity prices in Latin America and the Caribbean. Some links between China and Caribbean countries already exist as China and Taiwan seek allies, and UN votes, in the region by assisting with economic development programmes. Both Grenada and Dominica have courted Chinese and Taiwanese investment. China and Cuba are ideological friends, and there is potential for a growing relationship. China sees the Caribbean as an area of possibilities. As the Cricket World Cup approaches in 2007 the People's Republic of China is financially aiding the construction of new cricket facilities in Antigua, Grenada and Jamaica. The Chinese are discovering the value of dollar diplomacy. Meanwhile, as noted, the US pays less attention to the Caribbean region, focusing on the Middle East and Afghanistan.

Chapter 4

Politics since World War II

Since World War II the Caribbean islands have experienced a variety of government types and political orientations, ranging from right-wing dictatorships, to communist regimes, to liberal democracies, to dependent states. Commentators generalize about Caribbean politics at their peril, although politicians in the region face similar problems of achieving economic and social stability. Many British colonies won independence after several hundred years of European control, while smaller British islands remain connected to the United Kingdom. French and Dutch former colonies developed closer links with metropolitan centres, but gained internal self-governance. The United States continues to play a dominant role in the Caribbean, maintaining control in Puerto Rico and the US Virgin Islands and a strong presence in the region as a whole, including a military base/prison at Guantánamo Bay, Cuba. The Dominican Republic has moved from authoritarianism to limited democracy, while Haiti has proved difficult to govern effectively or peacefully. In Cuba, communist leader Fidel Castro replaced right-wing dictator Fulgencio Batista, and put in place a communist system. Castro is the longest running political leader in the western hemisphere, in office continuously since 1959. He governs with his younger brother, Raúl, and has seen ten US Presidents in power in Washington, DC, from Dwight D. Eisenhower to George W. Bush.

In 1945, at the close of World War II, the European empires in the Caribbean – French, Dutch and British – were intact, if substantially weakened. During the war France and the Netherlands were overrun by Germany, but their Caribbean colonies did not fall into German hands. The French territories were administered by the Vichy regime. The Netherlands' colonies reported to their government and Queen Wilhemena, in exile in London. Several Dutch corporations, fearing German takeover, moved assets to the Antilles, starting some of the islands, such as Curaçoa, on a career in offshore banking. As the War ended both France and the Netherlands moved to incorporate their Caribbean territories into the central metropolitan political framework. Assimilation had always been the preferred French political policy, and so, very quickly in 1946, after plebiscites in Guadeloupe and Martinique approved the idea of political union with France, the two territories became French overseas *départements*, with the same status as *départements* in France. People in Martinique and Guadeloupe became French citizens. In Martinique, Aimé Césaire, famous poet and Marxist, was politically active. Disappointed with post-war economic and social progress in the islands, he, and his Progressive Party, pushed for greater autonomy, but a 1962 referendum in the islands revealed a majority of residents in favour of the status quo.

Today, the citizens of Martinique and Guadeloupe are represented in Paris in the National Assembly (by four deputies) and in the Senate (by two senators). The local government of each island is administered by a directly elected General Council and a Regional Council. Local mayors and Council members run island politics. Both Guadeloupe and Martinique are relatively prosperous with the help of subsidies from the EU and France, good social services, access to EU markets and an outlet for migrants to the European Union. There are tensions, some racially charged, between locals and Europeans. Both territories are in the European Union and use the Euro as currency. Their postal addresses are designated 'France'!

The Netherlands Antilles (Aruba, Bonaire, Curaçao, St Maarten, St Eustatius and Saba) gained internal self-government in 1954, becoming an integral part of the Kingdom of the Netherlands, with equal status to Holland. The head of state is the sovereign of the Netherlands, represented by a governor. The Dutch would have liked their Antillean colonies to proceed from federation to independence (Suriname became independent in 1975), but that was not to be. Aruba has contemplated independence, and, in 1986, resenting what was felt to be dominance from Curaçao, separated from the Netherlands Antilles group, but remains an autonomous part of the Kingdom. St Maarten has followed Aruba's example. Periodically, referenda are held in the islands to determine the political will of the people. Choices put before the electorate include full autonomy, unification with the Netherlands, complete independence or a continuation of the current relationship of equal partnership within the Kingdom. Recent votes indicate that most people want the status quo to continue, meaning that the Netherlands Antilles should remain within the Kingdom of the Netherlands, although there is a desire that the Dutch respect their Caribbean countrymen and women more.

At the end of World War II, in terms of the number of islands, the British Empire had a significant presence in the Caribbean. To confirm the fact, empire postage stamps of many islands, including Jamaica, Trinidad and Barbados, displayed the crown of the British monarch. Sixty years later, in 2006, ten former British colonies have become independent, and island stamps colourfully depict local flowers, birds and scenery, plus symbols of national pride. The ten independent countries of Antigua-Barbuda, the Bahamas, Barbados, Dominica, Grenada, Jamaica, St Kitts-Nevis, St Lucia, St Vincent and the Grenadines, and Trinidad and Tobago, joined Haiti, the Dominican Republic and Cuba as sovereign states with representation in the United Nations.

Several small islands decided to remain as dependent territories associated with the United Kingdom. These include Anguilla, the British Virgin Islands, Montserrat, the Turks and Caicos Islands, and the Cayman Islands, with a total population of about 100,000. It was felt that these areas were too small and too vulnerable economically to stand alone as independent nation states. Interestingly, some of these islands have carved out economic niches in offshore services, performing relatively well economically and in terms of quality of life for their citizens. They join a few other territories such as Bermuda, the Falkland Islands (Malvinas) and Gibraltar as the last remnants of the British Empire. In 2002 inhabitants of British overseas territories in the Caribbean received full UK citizenship, with residency rights in the UK.

THE WEST INDIES FEDERATION (1958–62)

In 1958, on the road to de-colonization, the British colonial office experimented with a proposal to link its Caribbean colonies in the West Indies Federation (WIF), which involved Jamaica, Trinidad, Barbados and some small islands in the Lesser Antilles. Although it did not happen, it was hoped that British Guyana and British Honduras (now Belize) would also join the federation. After some debate the Federation capital was placed in Port of Spain in Trinidad, although Jamaicans, with over half the population of the Federation, were not pleased. Elections were held in 1958 and Grantley Adams of Barbados became prime minister of the Federation. Based on island population numbers, 45 members were elected to a House of Representatives. The Senate consisted of 19 nominated members.

The idea of federating several colonies with the objective of making units more economically stable and efficient before proceeding to independence was not limited to the Caribbean. A similar experiment was carried out with the creation of the Central African Federation between 1953 and 1963. It involved the British colonies of Southern Rhodesia (Zimbabwe), Northern Rhodesia (Zambia) and Nyasaland (Malawi), but it too ended in failure, with Zambia and Malawi becoming independent countries in 1964. Malaysia, federated in 1963, was successful, although Singapore left in 1965.

It is usually suggested that the West Indies Federation was 'doomed from the start'. Despite long negotiations (going back to discussion in the eastern Caribbean in 1932 and the Montego Bay conference of 1947), many in the Caribbean felt that the British government was trying to get the larger, more prosperous islands to oversee the smaller/poorer islands. In theory, the West Indies Federation had some good points, and was aimed at assisting the small, economically vulnerable islands make the transition to independent status in a larger, more efficient unit of government. In practice, the islands had little experience working together, and a lot of vocal island nationalism. Local particularism was prized, while the economic development and potential of islands differed. Jamaica and Trinidad had relatively large populations and resources. Jamaica had bauxite that attracted US investment and Trinidad had petroleum and natural gas. Other islands were tiny and lacked assets. Some wanted free movement of labour within the federation, which could pose problems for those islands that had more job opportunities, but most opposed open migration. Jamaica opposed a customs union.

A practical problem was that the executive power in the federal structure was weak. Health, education and trade remained in the hands of island legislatures and the Colonial Office. Tax-raising powers were also inadequate.[1] The situation was reminiscent of the weak US federal system under the Articles of Confederation, before the US Constitution was written in 1787. Another issue was that island leaders wanted recognition for their nations and themselves. Positions of power would be reduced in a federation.

In Jamaica, physically separated from others in the group, the WIF became a political issue, with Alexander Bustamante (JLP) opposed to the federation and his cousin Norman Manley (PNP) supporting it. In Trinidad, Prime Minister Eric Williams supported a strong federation. There was also tension between Jamaican views about federation and those of Trinidad's leaders. In 1961 a referendum was held in Jamaica that favoured withdrawal from the WIF by a vote of 54 to 46 per cent. Trinidad soon opted out, and the Federation was dissolved by the UK parliament in May 1962. Jamaica and Trinidad became independent that year. Barbados followed in 1966. Smaller Caribbean islands continued to cooperate as West Indies Associated States, until several became independent in the 1970s and '80s. It was part of a pattern in the Commonwealth whereby small and possibly economically vulnerable island colonies, such as Malta and Cyprus in the Mediterranean, became sovereign states. Today Malta and part of Cyprus are EU members.

One of the significant developments associated with the West Indies Federation was the creation of the University of the West Indies, a collaborative system of higher education with major campuses in Jamaica, Trinidad and Barbados. The institution helps to build a sense of unity and is a powerhouse of academic talent and energy.

The problem of federation among West Indian islands was highlighted by the case of Anguilla, a small island with about 10,000 inhabitants just a few miles from St Martin. Anguilla had been administratively linked with St Kitts and Nevis since the late nineteenth century, but was never satisfied with the arrangement. In 1958 Anguilla petitioned the governor to end the association. The request was denied. In 1967 Anguilla broke away from St Kitts and in a referendum Anguillians voted for separation. Two years later British paratroopers occupied the island and arbitration followed. No shots were fired. In 1980 Anguilla became a separate state, and is currently an overseas territory of the United Kingdom with internal autonomy.

INDEPENDENCE FOR THE ANGLO-CARIBBEAN

Like the original thirteen mainland American colonies, many islands in the Anglo-Caribbean, notably Barbados and Jamaica, have a history of representative government, involving a royal governor (representing the Crown), an appointed local Council (the Upper House) and an elected Assembly (the Lower House). Crucially, the Assembly (like the House of Commons in the UK) gained control of local revenues. The franchise (vote) to elect Assembly members was limited to landowners (predominantly white), but affluent locals could participate in government. In Barbados a representative system emerged in the early 1600s, and, after Jamaica was taken from Spain, its constitution of 1661 established the three-tier system of royal governor, appointed Council, and elected Assembly. Trinidad, acquired by Britain from Spain in the Napoleonic Wars, was given 'Crown Colony' government that did not include an elected Assembly.

With the exception of Barbados, Crown Colony government, involving direct British rule through appointed officials, became the norm in most islands. The shift from elected to appointed representatives began in Jamaica following the Morant Bay Uprising (1865), a hostile protest by black peasants facing economic hardship. Governor Eyre put down the rebellion with several hundred summary executions and floggings. Criticism followed, especially concerning the execution of George William Gordon, a middle-class mulatto and elected member of the Assembly. Governor Eyre was eventually dismissed and Crown

Colony government installed. The power of the white plutocracy was reduced and government from London was generally paternalistic. The system spread to other islands, except Barbados, which kept its Assembly. Crown Colony government was later modified. In Jamaica, in 1884, elected members (elected on a restrictive franchise) were added to the Legislative Council. Similar reforms occurred in other islands after World War I. Governors did not normally act against the wishes of elected members.

During the 1950s and '60s Jamaica, Trinidad and Tobago, and Barbados gained internal self-government and then won full independence. Not surprisingly given their political histories, the new countries adopted Westminster-style, parliamentary democracies, built around a two-chamber legislature (Upper and Lower Houses) and a two or three party system. Safeguards against the rise of dictators, and provisions for independent judiciaries, were included. Today each Lower House is elected by universal adult suffrage. Members of the Upper House are usually appointed. All, except the Republic of Trinidad and Tobago, have Elizabeth II as Head of State, who is represented by a Governor General, appointed on the advice of the local prime minister. As in Canada, the Governor General is a citizen of the country, performs ceremonial functions, and signs into law bills passed by the legislative branch. All the new Anglo-Caribbean nations opted to be members of the Commonwealth. Currently, politicians in several islands, including Jamaica and Barbados, are discussing changing the relationship with Britain by amending their constitutions and replacing the queen as head of state with a president. If this occurs the president would probably be head of state and the prime minister would exercise executive power, as is the case in Trinidad and Tobago.

Some commentators suggest that the Westminster-style of government has been 'Caribbeanized', meaning that personal power and patronage are emphasized in island politics.[2] Charismatic leaders are important. Political parties tend to be dominated by elites that insulate themselves from the masses. On the whole, the political systems in the Anglo-Caribbean work effectively and provide stability, even if problems of poverty and unemployment continue to plague island governments.

After independence the new Caribbean states wanted to translate political independence into economic independence. How could economies be stimulated and jobs created? How could health, education and social services be upgraded? These issues confronted local politicians, and remain at the forefront of contemporary Caribbean politics. Governments try to allocate a large proportion of revenue to the well-being of citizens.

Notice that the islands were moving to independence at the same time the UK was making a bid to enter what was then called the Common Market, now the European Union. The United Kingdom's first application to join the European Economic Community came in 1962. The French leader, General de Gaulle, vetoed the application in 1963 and did so again in 1967. The major problem for the Anglo-Caribbean was that their agricultural exports went mainly to the UK under Commonwealth agreements. What would be the impact if the UK were admitted to the EU? Would Caribbean sugar, bananas and other fruits pay exorbitant tariffs on entering Britain? Political independence might prove to be economically expensive. Could the Caribbean adjust to changing political and economic relationships?

The Anglo-Caribbean began to turn to regional neighbours for support. The creation of CARIFTA (Caribbean Free Trade Area) in 1968 called for free trade between member states, including most of the Anglo-Caribbean islands, although intra-Caribbean trade was small. The Caribbean Development Bank, with headquarters in Barbados, was established in 1969 with the aim of helping economic development in the region. Subsequently, newly independent Caribbean countries became members of the Organization of American States (OAS) and the Inter-American Development Bank (then the oldest and largest regional development institution in the world).

The late 1960s saw disturbances in the Caribbean, due to unemployment, increasing urbanization, inflation and rising expectations. The Caribbean was not alone. The year 1968 was one of student riots and sit-ins in Paris and Berkeley. Unrest in the Caribbean reflected the unequal nature of society, as working people felt they were not gaining ground. In Jamaica, university students, radicalized by 'Black Power' sentiment, marched against the administration's decision to ban the activist professor Dr Walter Rodney (1942–1980) from returning to Jamaica after attending a conference in Canada. Born in Guyana, a scholarship student at the University College, Jamaica, and then the School of Oriental and African Studies, London, Rodney gained a history doctorate at London University in 1966. He taught in Tanzania before moving to the University of the West Indies in Mona, Jamaica. His most famous book is *How Europe Underdeveloped Africa* (1972). Rodney challenged post-independence politics and the status quo, wanting to involve the masses in government. After three deaths and considerable destruction of property in the so-called Rodney Riots of 1968, the Jamaican military was sent in and order restored. Rioting, fuelled by high unemployment, also broke out in Willemstad, the capital of Curaçao, in 1969. The next year Trinidad was hit with disorder and arson. 'Black power' leaders were implicated in this radical era affected by the Vietnam War. Walter Rodney was assassinated with a bomb in Georgetown, Guyana, in 1980.

JAMAICA

Jamaican politics in the 1970s took a turn to the left. New Caribbean nations tried to assert their independence and develop economies by following socialist policies. Most notable was Jamaica's leader, Michael Manley (son of Norman), whose People's National Party (PNP) won elections in 1972 and again in 1976. He was a charismatic leader and engaging intellectual, opposed to colonialism, capitalism and imperialism. He tried to follow an independent economic policy with a strong anti-imperialist bent and became a spokesman for Third World issues. Manley espoused 'democratic socialism' and wanted to steer a middle way between reliance on western capitalism and Soviet communism, while maintaining democratic structures. Some businesses and banks were nationalized and land reform begun. He was especially opposed to the power of large overseas multinational corporations, and levied a new tax on foreign bauxite companies, such as Alcoa and Alcan, operating in the island. Revenue increased. Manley was friendly with Fidel Castro who visited Jamaica in 1977, making the United States annoyed and nervous about the direction politics was heading. It appears that the CIA tried to undermine the Manley government.[3]

The 1970s witnessed an oil crisis when petroleum was in short supply and prices high. The circumstances made it difficult for Manley's PNP to deliver a robust economy, and, although Manley won the 1976 election, political violence increased. In the 1980 election the more conservative Edward Seaga of the JLP won convincingly, and moderated the socialist programme. Seaga, of Syrian heritage, was more pro-US and urged President Reagan to devote resources to Caribbean development programmes. The Caribbean Basin Initiative (CBI), a US assistance package, was launched in the early 1980s and Jamaica benefited.

Michael Manley's People's National Party was back in power in the 1990s but radical socialism was out. Economic policies focused on increasing manufacturing and tourism, and friendly relations with the United States. Manley, experiencing poor health, stepped down in 1992, to be replaced by P. J. Patterson of the PNP, who won subsequent elections and, midway through his third five-year term, retired in the spring of 2006, to be replaced by the first female prime minister, Portia Simpson-Miller.

GRENADA

Another experiment with socialism – this time revolutionary socialism – occurred in Grenada between 1979 and 1983. As noted in chapter Three, Sir Eric Gairy, who first emerged as head of a trade union in the 1950s and then led the Grenada United Labour Party, held power for almost 30 years. Gairy superintended Grenada's independence in 1974. He exercised personal rule with mass support, using patron–client linkages. A paramilitary group (the Green Beasts) and the Mongoose Gang (a secret police) carried out acts of repression.

In 1979, with Grenada suffering economic depression and extremely high unemployment, a leading opposition group, the New Jewel Movement, seized power in a bloodless coup and established the People's Revolutionary Government (PRG) headed by Maurice Bishop

(1944–1983). Bernard Coard was Minister of Finance. The PRG turned away from the capitalist road to development, wanting to establish 'participatory democracy' within a one-party system. Employing a Marxist-Leninist approach, the group collaborated with Castro's Cuba and tried to forge trade links with countries in the Soviet bloc. The party's development platform involved building a bigger airport facility to service the tourist industry, and improving health, education and welfare with government funds.

By 1983 the Grenadine economy was in desperate straits. Bishop went to the IMF for financial assistance, angering extreme members of the PRG, notably Bernard Coard. Militant party members arrested Bishop, executed him, and burnt his body at Fort George, overlooking the sea-filled, volcanic crater that forms St George's Harbour, the main port of Grenada. Shortly afterwards the United States invaded Grenada (with token Caribbean units) to end the experiment in revolutionary socialism. Requests for US intervention came from several Caribbean Commonwealth leaders, most notably Eugenia Charles, the prime minister of neighbouring Dominica, who feared expansion of revolutionary activity. The fact that Charles did not go to the old colonial power, Britain, reflected the changed geopolitical situation. After the US invasion of Grenada the island returned to a capitalist path with foreign investment in tourism, completion of the enlarged airport and substantial US aid.

Elsewhere, politics in the 1980s were relatively conservative, with Edward Seaga in Jamaica, Tom Adams in Barbados, Eugenia Charles in Dominica and John Compton in St Lucia. They all followed neo-liberal, free-market policies and courted US aid. In 1981 the Organization of Eastern Caribbean States was established, linking seven small territories – Dominica, St Kitts-Nevis, Antigua-Barbuda, Grenada, St Lucia, Montserrat and Grenada – dedicated to economic integration and good government. All use the Eastern Caribbean dollar, and cooperate in judicial, defence and disaster-related affairs. Economic problems deepened in the 1980s, frequently referred to as the 'lost decade' for Latin America and the Caribbean. Governments had borrowed lavishly in the 1970s, but, with inflation and increasing interest rates, found it difficult to service high-interest debt in the 1980s. Additionally, recession in North America and Europe meant less demand for commodities, and fewer tourists. To meet interest payments unpopular austerity measures – known as structural adjustment policies or SAPs – including tax increases, government spending cuts and currency devaluations, were enforced to comply with IMF requirements. Unemployment rose, living standards dropped and discontent spawned riots in islands such as Jamaica in 1985.

TRINIDAD AND TOBAGO

In Trinidad and Tobago Prime Minister Dr Eric Williams (1911–1981) was leader of the People's National Movement (PNM) between 1956 and 1981. Williams, a historian trained at Oxford University, published his well-known *Capitalism and Slavery* in 1944, suggesting an economic motive for the abolition of the slave trade and slavery. When in power he tried a 'state capitalist' approach to economic development, using profits from the oil and gas industry to buy foreign-owned assets. He embarked on a policy of 'industrialization by invitation' to promote iron and steel, and chemical industries that used domestic petroleum inputs. The objective was to reduce imports and build an industrial base. Oil revenue would pay for social services and subsidize state-owned industries. Mighty Sparrow called the policy 'Capitalism Gone Mad' in a popular calypso.[4] Results were disappointing.

By 1983 Trinidad and Tobago was in debt; austerity measures and devaluation of the currency followed. The poor suffered most. There was widespread discontent with IMF-imposed adjustment measures that badly affected the underprivileged. In 1990 an armed Muslim group – *Jamaat al Muslimeen* – held Prime Minister A.N.R. Robinson and other politicians hostage in parliament. Several people were killed and Port of Spain erupted in violence and looting. The extremists surrendered after several days, and politics settled back into the usual pattern, with economic policies firmly in the neo-liberal camp. In the mid-1990s a politician of East Indian heritage, Basdeo Panday of the United National Congress Party, became prime minister, ending the dominance of the predominantly Afro-Caribbean People's National

Movement. The PNM was returned to power in 2002. Tourism has been promoted, especially upscale vacations for Europeans in Tobago. With recent high prices for oil and gas the Trinidadian economy is relatively buoyant, but the multi-ethnic character of the population challenges political unity.

BARBADOS

Barbadian politicians have chosen a relatively conservative path to economic development with positive results. The two major political parties, the Barbados Labour Party (BLP) and the Democratic Labour Party (DLP), share ideals concerning the development of a stable democracy committed to improving the quality of life for Bajans, as Barbadians are known. Power has changed hands in a responsible and civil fashion. In the last election of 2003 the BLP won with 55.8 per cent of the votes. Governments have stressed careful planning, management and fiscal responsibility. Both parties work with the Central Bank of Barbados to encourage foreign investment in tourism, offshore services and light manufacturing. Political stability has been the cornerstone of economic success, as revealed in the Human Development Index, where Barbados currently ranks 29th in the world, with the highest score in Latin America and the Caribbean (see Table 4).

Westminster-style democratic structures initially worked well in the Anglo-Caribbean, especially when compared with colonial zones in Africa. The parliamentary system gives governments control over both executive and legislative branches and means that government policies can be enacted. One explanation for success may lie in the islands' history: a long period of colonial rule in which legislative bodies developed, followed by a gradual process of de-colonization when well-defined political parties emerged, supported by trade unions and civic organizations. In addition, many Anglo-Caribbean governments, including in Barbados, have delivered good education, health care and social services to citizens, and have won support.

After World War II the reformist government of President Dumarsais Estime held power in Haiti between 1946 and 1950. François Duvalier (1907–1971), a physician who had done research on malaria, served as Director of Public Health and then Secretary of Labour under Estime, who was followed by several corrupt military regimes. In 1957 Duvalier, known as 'Papa Doc', was elected president, but in 1964 he changed the constitution. He was now 'President for life' and could name his successor. He ruled as a dictator with the help of his brutal private militia known as the *Tontons Macoutes*, a Creole term for bogeymen. Thousands died in Duvalier's terror campaign to silence opposition. Many professionals left for Montréal and elsewhere. His son, Jean Claude ('Baby Doc'), succeeded in 1971 and continued the corruption and oppression. He was eventually forced into exile in 1986 in France, being replaced by corrupt military governments.

In 1991 Jean-Bertrand Aristide (1953–), a Roman Catholic priest of left-wing persuasion, won the presidential election with widespread mass support, especially of the urban and rural poor. The military and mulatto elite were suspicious of his political intentions, and he lasted less than a year before another military coup ejected him. Aristide left the country, as did hundreds of 'boat people' bound for the US. The possibility of a refugee crisis encouraged President Clinton to act, and in 1994 Aristide was returned to power in a bloodless action by the US military and a small UN force. René Preval succeeded Aristide in 1995, the first democratic transfer of power in Haitian history. Preval grappled with financial problems and tried to develop links with Cuba. In 2001 Aristide was elected president again with a huge majority but has since been forced/persuaded out of office by internal violence and US pressure, and gone into exile. In 2006 UN peacekeepers from South American countries try to keep the peace, but drug gangs are heavily involved in Haiti and the island is in severe crisis, with no end in sight. An election with over 30 presidential candidates, held in February 2006, eventually named René Preval as president after UN involvement. Preval has a monumental task ahead. It is not clear if Aristide will return to Haiti.

DOMINICAN REPUBLIC

If Haiti is the worst-case scenario in the Caribbean, the Dominican Republic appears to be one of the best – stable and with a democratic structure in place, following years of dictatorship and corruption. The system is modelled after that of the United States. The president is elected for four years but cannot serve consecutive terms. The two-chamber Congress is composed of a Senate and a Chamber of Deputies. There are three major parties – the Dominican Revolutionary Party (PRD), the Dominican Liberation Party (PLD) and the Social Christian Reform Party (PRSC). In 2006 the Dominican Liberation Party held power.

After the assassination of dictator Trujillo in 1961, the left-leaning Juan Bosch, of the Dominican Revolutionary Party, won election to the presidency. He lasted a few months before a military coup ejected him from office. The military, the elite and elements in the United States' government feared that the Dominican Republic was heading the way of Cuba. In 1965, after a popular attempt to restore Bosch to the presidency led to violence, the US intervened with troops. The outcome was that, when elections were held in 1966, Joaquín Balaguer (who had been associated with Trujillo) won as leader of the Social Christian Reform Party. Pro-American and a right-winger, he was president until 1978, with the help of election fraud.

In 1978 the PRD was again in power, with Antonio Guzmán, a wealthy landowner, as president. The election was not without incident. When it appeared that Guzmán was going to win, pro-Balaguer troops intervened. A coup looked imminent, but the Carter administration threatened to stop US aid, and Guzmán won the vote count. In 1982 he was succeeded by PRD candidate Salvador Jorge Blanco. The reformist party tried to put in place social programmes and improve the standard of living for the masses, but ran into the debt crisis of the early 1980s. Loans from the IMF were conditional on spending cuts and other austerity measures which, as in Jamaica, led to rioting. Balaguer was back in office after the 1986 election, and won again in 1990 and 1994. He finally stepped aside two years later due to US pressure regarding fraud and corruption. Since 1996 elections have been clean and democracy appears to be functioning effectively. Economic growth was good until the 2003 economic downturn. The economy recovered in 2005 but income disparity and unemployment remain problematic.

CUBA

Cuba has a communist constitution that was formalized in 1976. Direct elections to the Assembly were allowed in 1992, and ten years later, in 2002, the socialist system was made 'irrevocable'. The Legislative branch of government, the National Assembly of Peoples' Power, meets twice a year and consists of 609 deputies elected for five-year terms by universal suffrage. Trade unions and other organizations make up lists of eligible political candidates. The National Assembly elects a 31-member Council of State. The president of this group is Head of State and nominates his Council of Ministers. Since 1976 Fidel Castro has been president, re-elected in 1998 and again in 2003, with 100 per cent of the legislative vote. Castro's younger brother, Raúl Castro Ruz (the designated successor to Fidel), is first vice-president of state and the Council of Ministers, and Castro's deputy. Although Cuban politicians describe their political system as a 'people's democracy', there is none of the freedoms associated with democracy, such as freedom of assembly, freedom of speech and freedom of the press. The media is controlled by government officials, and access to the Internet is restricted.

In 1980, amid political and economic discontent, thousands of Cubans demanded to leave the island. President Carter obliged by offering to take in refugees, resulting in the Mariél boat lift. Over 100,000 Cubans, including criminals and the mentally ill, landed in Florida from the port of Mariél. The communist regime got rid of undesirables, some of whom were not welcome in the US.

Cuba tries to follow an independent political and economic policy and remains actively opposed to US hegemony in the region. Cuba's communist, centrally planned economy has managed to survive, despite the US embargo and the end of Soviet financial aid and trade support in 1990. Adjustments were made to encourage tourism, make trade freer and permit small businesses to operate. The US dollar was legalized and foreign investment allowed in some state enterprises, such as tourism and the telephone system. But Castro has survived the Soviet collapse, and has overturned some adjustment policies. For example, the dollar is no longer legal tender. With the help of petroleum from President Chávez of Venezuela, Castro's political system remains intact. US relations with Cuba have not improved and the US continues an economic embargo, even though US relations with communist China and Vietnam have normalized. This may be because of Cuba's proximity to the US, the presence of Castro in continuous power since 1959, and political pressure from Cuban exiles in Florida, whose governor is Jeb Bush, brother of George W. Bush. In the US election of 2000 George W. narrowly won the presidency after a contentious and contested vote count in Florida that was eventually decided in the Supreme Court. The anti-Castro Cuban community in Florida is a significant voting bloc.

PUERTO RICO

Although Puerto Rico is not independent, it is self-governing in domestic affairs, with foreign policy and defence in US hands. The democratic system is modelled after that of the United States with a Senate as the Upper House and a House of Representatives. Puerto Ricans are US citizens, but are not directly represented in the US Congress. If resident in the US, and registered to vote, they can take part in federal elections. They do not pay federal income taxes if resident in the island. Puerto Ricans are eligible for federal aid, including food stamps, but males can also be drafted into the military. In 1947 the governor's position was made elective, and Puerto Rico became a 'Commonwealth' – *Estado Libre Asociado* – with a new constitution, in 1952. Not all Puerto Ricans were happy with the arrangement, and in 1954 some members of the Nationalist Party shot five Congressmen in the House of Representatives in Washington, DC.

The biggest political issue is whether Puerto Rico will become the 51st state in the union. In the most recent plebiscite of 1998 over 50 per cent of the population was in favour of continuing the commonwealth relationship. Approximately 46.5 per cent supported statehood, and a small minority of about 2.5 per cent wanted independence. Statehood would affect manufacturing jobs and industry because tax advantages would end and Puerto Ricans would pay federal income taxes.

Puerto Ricans are proud of their Spanish heritage, cherishing Spanish culture, history and language. A large percentage (perhaps as high as 60 per cent) of the population does not speak English. It is interesting to note that Puerto Rico has its own Olympic team, illustrating the desire for a separate identity on the world stage.

Most countries in the Caribbean region are democratic with orderly transfers of power. Political dialogue and criticism are allowed. Haiti struggles to establish a democratic system, and Cuba lacks free speech, free association and a free press. External influences, especially from the United States, whether military, political or economic, have a significant impact on politics in the whole area, and each island nation tries to maintain a sense of independence. Since the collapse of the Soviet Union, US attention has shifted from fear about the spread of communism to concern about illegal drugs and migration.

Many in the Caribbean feel their quality of life is not improving, and external pressure from the US, IMF and World Bank to tighten economic policy and cut back on spending is blamed for hard times. Some, especially the young, are frustrated with the political system because they feel impotent. The percentage of citizens voting in elections is not high. People want jobs and an end to depressed economic conditions. There are powerful critics of IMF and World Bank policies, policies that promote free trade. Opening small economies to competition from major multi-national corporations can be damaging; small island businesses just cannot compete. Frequently, competition results in the closing of local manufacturing plants. Sometimes investment by major corporations, in tourism for example, can create jobs in construction and the service sector. But, in the area of food production, cheap, subsidized agricultural produce from North America and the EU results in curtailment of local agriculture.[5]

Chapter 5

Economies

Before 1960 most Caribbean economies focused on agriculture. Islands relied on agricultural exports to generate foreign exchange. Most jobs were in agriculture, and most people lived in rural areas. Sugar cane, grown largely on coastal plantations, and bananas were the major export crops, although coffee, cocoa, fruits, coconuts, tobacco and spices were also shipped abroad. Many smallholders grew crops on farm plots, frequently under 5 acres, to help feed their families and to sell in local markets. Ranchers in a few islands, such as the Dominican Republic, Cuba and Puerto Rico, raised livestock, and many people kept poultry.

Today, agriculture is declining everywhere in the Caribbean. In many islands agricultural production equals less than 5 per cent of Gross Domestic Product (GDP). Although employment in agriculture is still relatively high in some islands, notably Jamaica and Haiti, most islands import large amounts of expensive food, mainly from the United States. Livestock industries, involving cattle, pigs, goats and poultry, are significant in the Greater Antilles.

In the contemporary Caribbean the service sector, especially tourism, has transformed island economies, providing most of the jobs and contributing most to GDP. Tourism is the major driving force in the majority of Caribbean economies. Newer service industries, such as offshore banking and insurance, are also growth areas. Industrialization has occurred in some of the larger islands, notably Puerto Rico, Cuba, the Dominican Republic, Trinidad and Jamaica. Manufacturing operations, mainly involving garments, are supported in some islands by tax incentives and the creation of free trade zones. For example, in the Dominican Republic more than 40 industrial free trade zones operate, many involved in textile production for export to US markets.

Caribbean economies are on the periphery of the world trade system, and depend on the United States and Europe for markets, investment, credit and aid. The region imports more than it exports, and, because the prices of most exports are lower than the prices of imports, deficits and indebtedness result. Debt as a percentage of GDP is high in many islands. Servicing debt is expensive and stultifies economic growth. There are exceptions, such as petroleum production in Trinidad, but on the whole the Caribbean does not produce much that is competitive in world markets. With its proximity to the North American market, the Caribbean can provide economical vacations.

PRIMARY ECONOMIC SECTOR

Agriculture

The primary sector of any economy involves activities, such as farming, forestry, fishing and mining, that directly exploit natural resources. When the islands were European colonies sugar cane cultivation became the dominant economic activity, responsible for the development of the Atlantic slave trade. Sugar cane changed the face of the Caribbean landscape and people.

Although sugar cane is still grown on some islands, such as the Dominican Republic, Cuba, Trinidad, Jamaica and Barbados, the industry is losing profitability and declining. Barbadian sugar output went from a high in 1957 of 208,000 metric tons to 50,000 metric tons in 2001.[1] In the 1960s sugar occupied almost all the cultivable land. West and Augelli wrote: 'Nowhere else in the Caribbean has sugar reigned so long and absolutely, and nowhere else is its reign more secure.'[2] Today resorts and golf courses are expanding and sugar has lost its crown.

Several islands, such as Antigua and St Lucia, stopped growing sugar some time ago, and St Kitts closed the state-owned sugar business in

2005. The government-owned sugar industry in Cuba was the mainstay of Cuba's economic relationship with the Soviet Union. Cuban sugar was exchanged for Soviet petroleum until the collapse of the USSR in 1990, when the Cuban sugar harvest was reported at 8 million tons. Since then sugar production has declined in Cuba. The Cuban government has attempted to restructure agriculture away from sugar cane, and many state-run sugar mills have closed. The sugar harvest of 2005 was down to 1.3 million tons – the poorest harvest since 1908 – well below the target of 4 million tons! Drought was blamed for the shortfall. Other crops such as soybeans and maize are increasingly grown, and livestock and forestry operations promoted. In Cuban cities hand-watered urban vegetable gardens help to provide food.

Sugar production has declined for a number of reasons, including competition from other countries, the end of price supports, lack of modernization and a change of taste to corn syrup and artificial sweeteners. Competition from cheaper production areas, such as Brazil and Australia, is significant. Although India is the world's largest sugar producer, Brazil is the largest global exporter of sugar. Changing world trade regulations signal the death of sugar in the Caribbean. The European Union has long had an agreement with the former Caribbean colonies of Britain to import sugar quotas at favourable prices. Recently the World Trade Organization (WTO) declared this deal unfair. EU price supports are supposed to be phased out, further crippling the industry. Unless alternative uses, such as the production of ethanol for fuel, are developed, sugar will continue to lose ground. Recently, because of high oil prices, interest in ethanol has potentially breathed new life into sugar.

Growing sugar cane provided low-paying, hard, physical jobs. There was no incentive to educate workforces and little opportunity to advance in the industry beyond field labourer. The decline of sugar has come about because economies are diversifying, wages are rising and education and lifestyles are improving. In most of the contemporary Caribbean the decrease in sugar cultivation reflects progress, not depression.

Bananas have been an important export crop in several islands, including Jamaica, St Lucia, St Vincent, Dominica, Martinique and Guadeloupe. Today Caribbean banana growers, sometimes family-run farms, face stiff competition from cheaper growing areas in Central

America, and suffer from the phasing out of preferential trade agreements with the EU. The WTO has said that the EU preferential banana system is in breach of rules. Banana exports are consequently falling, especially from St Lucia, St Vincent and Grenada. One exception is that banana exports from Martinique, which as a member of the EU does not have to negotiate preferential treaties, are good. Both sugar and bananas face similar issues in a global market place. Caribbean producers just cannot compete with other areas around the world, as preferential trade agreements are challenged.

Other traditional crops, such as coffee and tobacco, are also declining. Coffee, grown on hill slopes mainly in the Greater Antilles, faces competition from Brazil and other Latin American countries, although local-grown coffee is consumed in domestic Caribbean markets. Tobacco is most significant in Cuba. Hand-rolled Havana cigars are world-famous. Cigarettes and cigars are also produced in the Dominican Republic. Some islands produce specialized crops, such as limes in Dominica, arrowroot (used for baby and invalid foods, and recently computer paper) in St Vincent, nutmeg in Grenada (the second largest producer after Indonesia), and allspice and yams in Jamaica.

In general, production costs for agricultural commodities in the Caribbean are too high to be competitive in world markets. One exception is marijuana (ganja), grown in several islands, although how much is difficult to document. Marijuana was introduced into Jamaica by indentured labourers from India, where it was used in the Hindu religion. Now grown in Jamaica (especially in the central Cockpit Country, the traditional home of runaway slaves) and other islands, marijuana enters the United States and Europe illegally.

Traditionally, many people in the Caribbean have small parcels of land where they grow food for family consumption. Kitchen gardens are common. A unique communal landownership custom, referred to as 'family land', developed in the Anglo-Caribbean after the Emancipation of slaves (1833–8). Ex-slaves bought small plots of land to show independence from planter control, and as a mark of freedom. Descendants of original owners have communal use of the land forever, even if no will survived. Land can be used for farming or housing, but should not be sold. Even if an heir migrates, rights to family land are retained.[3]

Forestry

Although most islands were forested before European contact, many forests have been cleared for agriculture and to provide timber. The case of Haiti (heavily involved in sugar production in the eighteenth century) is the most extreme, where less than 1 per cent of the land is in forest (see chapter One). A recent Environmental Sustainability Index ranked Haiti very near the bottom in the world in terms of pollution and abuse of natural resources. On the other side of the island in the Dominican Republic, although acreage in woodland is declining, about 25 per cent of land is still forested. Mahogany, satinwood, pine and cedar are grown. Mountainous Dominica, in the Lesser Antilles, is one of the most wooded islands with about 60 per cent of land in forest, a useful selling point for the development of eco-tourism. Tobago has a forest reserve dating from the eighteenth century. Cuba has valuable woods, such as mahogany and cedar, the latter used for cigar boxes.

Fishing

Most islands have a small fishing industry, mainly in marine waters, to cater to local and tourist demand. Cuba is one of the few Caribbean islands with an important export fishing industry, third in importance after sugar and nickel. Some islands specialize in a local catch, such as flying fish in Barbados and lobster in the Bahamas. On the whole, the fishing industry is not well developed due to lack of deep-water vessels and refrigeration capacity.

Mining

Cuba has an important mining sector with plentiful supplies of iron, and some chrome, cobalt, copper, manganese and marble. Cuba produces steel. The steel hardener, nickel, used in weapons production, is a strategic resource, and a significant export earner for Cuba. Recently,

Cuba's petroleum industry has grown rapidly, as oil companies from Brazil, Europe and Canada develop offshore resources.

Nickel, silver and gold are mined in the Dominican Republic. Although declining because of competition from other countries, Jamaica still exports both bauxite and alumina for the production of aluminium. The US and Canada are the major recipients, and final processing to aluminium usually takes place in North America because of high-energy demands. Jamaica also has gypsum and limestone in abundance.

Trinidad is the one island economy that runs on domestic oil and gas production. The state-owned company, Petrotrin, oversees the industry, which has allowed Trinidad to expand industrial production into heavy industries and petro-chemicals. Barbados also produces a small amount of oil for domestic consumption.

SECONDARY ECONOMIC SECTOR

The secondary sector involves industry, manufacturing and construction, and in the Caribbean only became significant after World War II. Today, most islands have small manufacturing plants involving food processing, beverages, cement and so on, catering to local consumption. Islands in the Greater Antilles and Trinidad have larger operations, with steel-making in the Dominican Republic and the manufacture of pharmaceuticals in Puerto Rico. In addition, oil is refined in Puerto Rico, Trinidad, Curaçao, Aruba, St Croix and the Bahamas, and St Lucia, St Eustatius and Bonaire have large trans-shipment terminals for oil heading to North American markets. Obviously, oil terminals and refineries pose environmental threats and do not sit well alongside tourist resorts.

Some commentators suggest that, long before the Industrial Revolution, Caribbean sugar production involved an industrial component, because, after harvesting and crushing, cane juice is boiled in a factory-like setting to produce molasses and semi-refined brown sugar. The notion of 'the factory in the field' encapsulates this idea. Sugar mills and boiling factories are still operating in some islands, notably

Cuba and the Dominican Republic, although much final refining to produce white sugar takes place outside the region in the US and Europe.

Rum and molasses (a thick syrup left after sugar juice has been boiled) are both exported, with significant amounts of rum shipped to the United States and Europe, particularly Britain. Rum manufacturing is a long established industry in the Anglo-Caribbean, where, even in mercantilist, colonial days, the British freely traded rum in the global marketplace. Rum and molasses were shipped to New England, mainly Massachusetts, where over 100 rum distilleries operated in the 1770s![4] In the eighteenth century a daily rum ration became part of the Royal Navy's regimen, helping to boost production in the islands. Mount Gay rum of Barbados is one of the oldest continuously operating producers, with records going back to 1703. Tourists can visit the premises. Interestingly, the rum industry was slow to develop in the Spanish and French islands because of royal laws against rum production to protect domestic wines and brandies. In Spanish territories liquor made from sugar cane (*aguardiente*), although drunk locally, was very rough and unpalatable, produced with poor distilling equipment. Rum, a drink for the lower classes, was smuggled into Spanish colonies from British islands.

Today, most islands have rum manufacturing plants that produce liquor for export, domestic consumption and the tourist industry. Offering rum to visitors is part of local hospitality. Every self-respecting island has its special version of 'planters' punch' made with local rum. Light, dry rums, such as those made by Bacardi, are produced in Puerto Rico and the US Virgin Islands. The Bacardi family originally started rum production in Cuba and, after a legal battle in the US courts in the 1930s, gained permission to open a plant in Puerto Rico. Bacardi rum gained duty-free access to the US market. It was a good plan; in 1960 Fidel Castro took over Bacardi operations in Cuba. The Bacardi empire has grown and thrived. Now Bacardi operations include Martini and Rossi, Dewars Scotch, Bombay gin, plus tequila, brandy, beer and vodka brands. In Puerto Rico Bacardi is one of the highest corporate taxpayers, employing many workers.

In Martinique most of the rum drunk is white. Rums such as Mount Gay in Barbados, Captain Morgan in Jamaica and El Presidente in the Dominican Republic are darker and heavier. Many distilleries, including those in Puerto Rico, the Virgin Islands, Barbados and St Kitts, import molasses (increasingly from Brazil and the Dominican Republic) for rum production. A further by-product of sugar is bagasse, the fibre left after juice extraction, which is used to fuel boilers and to make wallboard. Ethanol can also be produced from sugar, and, as already noted, may become more important as a fuel source. Early in 2006 sugar futures prices were at their highest levels in a quarter-century, linked to speculation about the possibilities of ethanol.

After World War II it was generally realized that Caribbean agricultural economies could not support growing populations or promote economic development, and plans were made to add manufacturing sectors to their economies. In 1947 'Operation Bootstrap' was launched in Puerto Rico by the US government. Tax incentives and low interest loans promoted investment. Puerto Rico's commonwealth relationship with the US enhanced its attractiveness, and many US companies (initially clothing and shoes) re-located operations to the island to take advantage of tax breaks and low labour costs. Heavy industry, electronics, oil refining, petrochemicals and, most recently, pharmaceuticals (Johnson & Johnson and Bristol-Myers) have followed. Economic growth rates were impressive during the 1950s, '60s and '70s, although unemployment was sometimes high. Profits were frequently sent to the mainland US. Puerto Rico now has the most industrialized economy in the Caribbean, but is heavily dependent on the US for capital investment, credit, trade and federal subsidies. Unemployment continues to be a problem and too many people live in poverty. Food stamps help families survive but breed a sense of dependency. Migration to the US provides a safety-valve. Tax exemptions for corporations operating in Puerto Rico are due to run out in 2006/7, and, if not renewed, the Puerto Rican economy will face adjustment problems. Puerto Rico's political relationship with the US limits the island's economic interests in the wider Caribbean.

In the English-speaking Caribbean economic thinkers like Sir Arthur Lewis of St Lucia (parents from Antigua) generated ideas to promote economic development. Lewis was educated at LSE before appointment to a professorship at Manchester University in 1948 at the age of 33. He worked on development economics in the British Colonial Office, concluding that labour could be diverted from the stagnant agricultural sector to a new dynamic Caribbean manufacturing sector. *The Theory of Economic Growth* (1955) is his most famous work. Knighted in 1963, he went on to Princeton, before setting up the Caribbean Development Bank in Barbados. In 1979 Lewis was awarded the Nobel Prize in Economics. He promoted Caribbean manufacturing and industrialization by a system known as 'industrialization by invitation', which relied on attracting foreign capital to finance development while protecting domestic operations. In mainland Latin America many governments used similar policies known as Import Substitution Industrialization (ISI) that sought to protect home industries with high tariffs in order to shield local manufacturers from cheaper imports. The goal was economic independence from core capitalist countries in Europe and the US. A whole academic industry was built up around the concept known as 'dependency theory'.

In the 1960s and '70s some countries in the Caribbean, like Jamaica under Prime Minister Michael Manley, tried to follow socialist policies, promoting government-run industries that aimed at self-reliance. The socialist approach, together with policies of 'industrialization by invitation', came to an end in the 1980s with the debt crisis, when Caribbean governments that had earlier borrowed heavily (and most had) could not repay loans because of increasing interest rates. Forced to reschedule payments and negotiate with international lenders like the World Bank and International Monetary Fund (IMF), governments in the Caribbean had little choice but to shift to policies known as neo-liberalism. This involves freer trade, opening domestic markets, privatizing economic activity, export-led development (especially non-traditional exports) and conservative spending policies in relation to social services. The World Bank and IMF demanded such structural adjustment policies (SAPS), which were not popular with island politicians or populations. Most Caribbean countries today follow neo-liberal strategies, but foreign debt continues to be an issue, especially in Haiti and Jamaica.

Many Caribbean governments, notably the Dominican Republic and Jamaica, have added manufacturing operations by creating export-processing zones, where businesses import raw materials, such as textiles or electronic parts, and local workers assemble materials that are then exported as finished products, usually to the US. These types of assembly plants, referred to as *maquiladoras*, usually employ low wage, non-unionized females. Island governments offer tax incentives and infrastructure to attract manufacturers and jobs, but they are not always successful, largely because global companies seek the most competitive wages and will move operations to lower wage areas such as China.

TERTIARY OR SERVICE SECTOR

Since the 1960s the service sector, including government jobs, has grown to become the largest employer in the islands, typically involving well over half the workforce.

Tourism

Most Caribbean island economies are heavily dependent on the service sector, which includes travel and tourism, offshore services and government employment. Tourism is now the backbone of Caribbean economies and the leading earner of foreign exchange. Governments generally promote tourism to generate jobs in hotels, restaurants, travel services, retailing and construction. Tourism is a complex industry involving many activities from lodging to transportation, food services, construction, insurance, financial services and government agencies.

Before the 1960s Caribbean resorts served the affluent. The British upper classes went to Barbados, the French to Martinique, the Dutch to Curaçao. Wealthy or celebrity North Americans favoured Cuba or the Bahamas. Mass tourism developed in the 1960s with the rise of middle-class disposable incomes, package holidays and jet airliners. Initially Caribbean governments were skeptical about tourism. How could tourism be linked to wider development goals? Would the islands remain tied to the economic ups and downs of countries outside the region? A new dependency would develop – a new monoculture. Most island governments soon realized they had little option but to capitalize on Caribbean climates and beautiful scenery. Now governments promote and market their islands for the tourism industry, but attempt to focus on sustainable tourism, which involves careful planning, respecting input from local communities and considering environmental health.

The Caribbean is a commodity. Island destinations compete for tourists and many try to market special attractions. Some islands, such as the Bahamas, promote mass tourism with relatively cheap package holidays, entertainment and gambling. Other islands, for example the Cayman Islands, focus on exclusive resorts and yachting marinas for the very rich. Water-sport activities (sailing, snorkelling, scuba diving) are promoted and popular in many places. Eco-tourism is also attractive. New niches are developing in historical tourism, involving forts and plantation houses. Famous people who visited the Caribbean, such as Ernest Hemingway in Cuba or George Washington in Barbados, can generate a focal point for tourist interest. Cultural and archaeological holidays are appearing. Sex tourism and sports tourism are marketed. Creole festivals, calypso jamborees and Mardi Gras extravaganzas are popular. The World Cup Cricket Competition will take place in the Caribbean in 2007. There is something for everyone.

Most tourists to the Caribbean travel from the United States, with significant numbers arriving from Canada and Europe. US citizens favour the Bahamas and Puerto Rico but are prohibited from visiting Cuba as tourists by the US government. Although colonial links continue to influence European tourist choices because of language, culture and marketing, the Dominican Republic and Cuba are increasingly popular with Europeans in general. Frequently, visitors stay at purpose-built resort areas, such as Ocho Rios or Montego Bay in Jamaica, on the other side of the island from the slums of Kingston. International companies like Hilton and Marriott have built large hotel complexes along Caribbean coasts, creating what are in effect gated communities.

The tourist industry has grown rapidly. In 1990 there were about 10 million stay-over visitors in the Caribbean. The Caribbean Tourism Organization estimates that in 2004 that number grew to 21.8 million and that gross expenditure by the visitors was $21 billion. In 2004 the top five countries for stay-over tourist arrivals were the Dominican Republic (3,443,205), the Bahamas (1,450,037), Jamaica (1,278,921), Cuba (1,134,611) and Puerto Rico (1,082,649).[5]

Currently, Caribbean cruises are attractive, especially for North Americans anxious about terrorist attacks. Cruise ships can overtax small ports and towns in the Caribbean, and do not benefit local economies as much as visitors in hotels. In 2004 the five ports with most cruise passenger visits were Nassau in the Bahamas (3.4 million), St Thomas in the US Virgin Islands (2 million), San Juan in Puerto Rico (1.4 million), Cayman Islands (1.4 million) and St Maarten (1.3 million).[6] Total cruise passengers to the Caribbean, including Cancún and Cozumel, reached 20.5 million. As a tourist destination for Americans, the Caribbean has been favoured as prices in Europe appear higher. The Caribbean is also perceived to be a relatively safe region. Despite an overall decrease in travel after the 9/11 terrorist attacks, tourism to Caribbean destinations rebounded quite quickly. Obviously, the recent high price of oil is a major concern for the tourist industry as a whole, affecting everything from the cost of jet fuel, to taxi fares, to restaurant meals.

The tourist industry has drawbacks. It relies on economies in faraway places. A recession in the United States can reduce tourist arrivals. Local employment is seasonal and wages are usually low. Foreign corporations control much of the industry and dictate prices and terms of trade. Foreign currency frequently does not stay in the Caribbean, but buys imported items, including food, outside the region. Tourists are usually white, affluent people, and workers are usually blacks trying to make a living. In addition, environmental effects can be costly, especially in small islands with limited water resources. Beach erosion and marine pollution are constant concerns. Nevertheless, the bottom line is that tourist receipts generate tax revenue and stimulate economic growth. Foreign exchange is earned. The challenge is to link tourism into local activities such as food and beverage production, and to ensure careful management of the fragile environment that is the cornerstone of the entire industry. Caribbean governments and people should plan for long-term benefits rather than capitalize on short-term economic rewards.

Offshore services

Offshore financial services are significant in several islands, especially in small overseas dependencies that fly the British flag. The Cayman Islands, Anguilla, the British Virgin Islands, and Turks and Caicos Islands (whose residents are British citizens) offer a multitude of services, including banking, insurance and ship registration. These islands have advantages because the British connection provides stability and legality, language is not a problem and they are close to the United States. Other islands involved in offshore services include the Bahamas, Barbados, Nevis and the Netherlands Antilles. Many international corporations deposit funds in offshore banks, wishing to avoid high taxes in mainland countries. Some companies, such as Enron, were creative in establishing offshore subsidiaries that were not subject to US tax laws. Enron ran into financial difficulties and has gone bankrupt. Its officials received significant gaol terms.

Many Caribbean countries are concerned about tax evasion, money laundering, drug running and other criminal activities. States in the Caribbean want to ensure that offshore services are legal. Since the terrorist attacks of 11 September 2001, the United States in particular has tried to monitor and regulate global capital flows, especially in the strategically located Caribbean region.

Other offshore services that have developed in the Caribbean during the new age of global information technology include data processing, call centres, Internet commerce and telemarketing operations. Activities such as insurance claims and telephone billing are processed in some Caribbean islands. There have been mixed results, with the Jamaican experience (going from good to disappointing) being a cautionary tale. Although some islands have benefited greatly from service industries, wages can be low, control is exercised from outside the region and operations such as call centres can be moved more easily than assembly plants.

THE INFORMAL SECTOR

Drugs

It is estimated that a third of illegal drugs entering the United States, including marijuana, cocaine and heroin, passes through the Caribbean. Much of the production comes from Colombia, although there is some home-grown marijuana raised in the region, especially in the Cockpit Country of Jamaica. Illegal drugs and money laundering go hand in hand, leading to increased levels of crime and corruption.

Remittances

Many Caribbean economies benefit from remittances sent home to family members by migrants earning wages abroad, principally in North America or Europe. Remittances can be hard currency or material goods. Some Caribbean islands receive more economic assistance from remittances than from foreign aid programmes, and, generally speaking, remittances go into the hands of those relatives who can use the resources most effectively. Remittances not only allow families to purchase food and other necessities, they also generate capital to start small businesses and are used as savings. In 2003 remittances in millions of dollars from migrants in the US to the Dominican Republic was $2,217, to Jamaica $1,425, to Cuba $1,194, to Haiti $977 and to Trinidad and Tobago $88. In 2003 the average sent by each migrant in the US to Latin America and the Caribbean was $1,800. In 2004 total remittances to Latin America and the Caribbean was over $40 billion.[7]

TRADE AND ECONOMIC INTEGRATION

The Caribbean islands are heavily trade-dependent, and the US is the most significant partner for many islands, with the exception of Cuba. About one third of Jamaican exports go to the US, and approximately 40 per cent of its imports come from the US. Over 80 per cent of exports from the Dominican Republic go to the US, and over half imports come from there. There are exceptions. The Netherlands Antilles carries on a lot of trade with Venezuela (mostly petroleum). Guadeloupe and Martinique are connected to the European Union and most of their trade is with France. Exports from Barbados and other former British connected islands, such as St Lucia, go mostly to the UK. Cuba's trade partners are currently diverse, with significant exports going to the Netherlands, Canada and Russia, in that order. Imports to Cuba arrive from Spain, Venezuela, Italy, the US (food and medicine, despite the embargo), China and elsewhere. Historically, inter-island trade has been low, but is increasing. Trinidad is developing links with other islands such as Barbados and Jamaica, and Caribbean exports to Latin America are growing.

Economic cooperation and integration, although economically sensible, are not easy in the Caribbean because of localism, competition, diverse levels of development and small markets. Currently, CARICOM (the Caribbean Community and Common Market), established in 1973 and with approximately 6 million people today, tries to move towards more cooperation (such as the West Indies Shipping Corporation), but has not developed a common market. It does not have a common external tariff or free movement of labour – both objectives for the future. Members of CARICOM are Antigua-Barbuda, the Bahamas, Barbados, Belize, Dominica, Grenada, Guyana, Jamaica, Montserrat, St Kitts-Nevis, St Lucia, St Vincent, Suriname, and Trinidad and Tobago. Associate members are the British Virgin Islands, Turks and Caicos, Anguilla and the Caymans. Several territories, such as the Dominican Republic, Mexico, Venezuela and the Netherlands Antilles, have observer status. CARICOM uses the Caribbean Forum (CARIFORUM) to negotiate with the EU on trade and economic development. Haiti, the Dominican Republic and, most recently, Cuba, have membership in CARIFORUM, and efforts are being made to ensure regional integration and cooperation.[8]

The Association of Caribbean States (ACS), which includes CARICOM members plus Mexico, Central America and the Dominican Republic, also seeks to promote economic cooperation in the wider Caribbean. Caribbean countries are excluded from NAFTA (the North American

Free Trade Agreement), but there is discussion of a Free Trade Area of the Americas (FTAA), which would include Caribbean states. However, such an organization would further open Caribbean markets to imports from larger, more competitive, economies. It may be that a Caribbean Common Market, providing a degree of protection for small island industries, would be a better strategy. It is clear that the region would benefit from integration and cooperation to create a more competitive and sustainable community, with improved conditions for all. Economic integration can promote development and potentially uncover government mismanagement and corruption.[9]

THE CASE OF CUBA: SOCIALIST ECONOMY

Since the Revolution of 1959 Cuba has taken a unique path to development in the Caribbean. Castro followed socialist policies and allied Cuba with the Soviet bloc. The economy was diversified, but sugar continued to be its foundation, because sugar was exchanged for Soviet petroleum. Just as Puerto Rico was dependent on the US for economic stability, Cuba was dependent on the Soviet Union. Cuba borrowed heavily from the Soviets and amassed a huge debt. It also developed social services, notably in health care and education.

Since 1990 and the collapse of the Soviet empire, Cuba has suffered. Imports of Soviet oil, machinery, fertilizer and credit stopped. Food imports, such as grain, came to an end, affecting ordinary Cubans. Income and trade have been devastated. The 'special period in the time of peace' (as Castro dubbed the post-Soviet period of hardship) forced Cuba to adopt some neo-liberal policies in line with the rest of the Caribbean, including promoting tourism and courting foreign investment. The US dollar was legalized for a time. Farmers could sell surpluses on the market, and small business ventures, such as cafés, were allowed. Tourism, coming from Europe, Canada and Latin America, is currently the leading economic sector. Health tourism is also included in Cuba's offerings.

The US continues an economic embargo and encourages other countries to follow suit. The US Government prohibits American tourists from visiting the island. Countries such as Canada and Mexico have invested in Cuban enterprises, including tourism, mining and biotechnology.[10]

Recently, it looks as if Castro has found a friend and ally in Venezuela's Hugo Chávez, who, since the year 2000, has provided petroleum to Cuba on easy credit terms. Venezuela also buys Cuban goods, such as prefabricated housing, and pays cash for services rendered by Cuban doctors, technicians and teachers, who serve two- or three-year contracts in Venezuelan *barrios*. The Chávez government pays wages and deposits money into bank accounts in Cuba. Cuban professionals returning home fill the planes with consumer goods from Venezuela, ranging from cosmetics to refrigerators.

Chapter 6

People and Society

In 2006 the population of the Caribbean islands was about 40 million, despite high rates of emigration (see Table 3). The population had almost doubled since 1960. Population numbers vary greatly from island to island. Cuba has the most people with 11.3 million, while several island nations, including Dominica and Grenada, have populations of about 100,000. Population densities are high, with Barbados posting the highest island density of 1,554 people per square mile, although it currently has one of the lowest rates of population increase in the region, thanks to a successful family planning project started in the 1950s, a good education system and rising living standards. The overall rate of natural increase in the Caribbean region is declining, and at 1.1 per cent is below that of South America (1.5 per cent) and Central America (2.0 per cent). However, the Dominican Republic and Haiti have high rates of natural increase at 1.7 and 1.9 per cent respectively. The population of the island of Hispaniola (which includes Haiti and the Dominican Republic), currently at almost 17 million, is projected to be nearly 24 million by 2025. It is worth noting that in 1950 Haiti had a population of 3.1 million and the Dominican Republic only 2.1 million.[1] Everywhere in the Caribbean pressure on resources is serious and too many people seek scarce jobs. Unemployment and under-employment are common. As will be seen, migration (documented and otherwise) acts as a safety valve.

THE HUMAN DEVELOPMENT INDEX

The quality of life has improved steadily in many Caribbean islands, although there continues to be a significant gulf between the affluent and the poor. Infant mortality is declining, and incomes and life expectancy are rising in most countries, with the glaring exception of Haiti. Understanding that the well-being of people is not just about incomes, the United Nations has constructed a Human Development Index (HDI) to measure the well-being of societies around the world. The UN uses a composite of three indicators – life expectancy at birth, literacy and school enrolment, and Gross Domestic Product (GDP) per capita – to rank countries. The HDI links economic growth and quality of life, trying to assess how effectively resources are used in regard to health and education. Table 4 shows the HDI for the countries of the Caribbean. There is variability within the region, ranging from Barbados, ranked 29 in the world, to Haiti at 153. Barbados's success seems to be derived from good foreign exchange earnings, generated by tourism and offshore services. A relatively high percentage of revenue has flowed into improving health and education. Since independence from Britain in 1966 political parties have practised sound public administration, generating a sense of stability that encourages foreign investment.[2] The quality of government is important. Barbados also has a sizeable expatriate population from Britain and many return migrants from the UK who have chosen to retire to their home island, avoiding the frost and clouds of British winters.

Six countries – Barbados, St Kitts-Nevis, the Bahamas, Cuba, Trinidad and Tobago, and Antigua-Barbuda – are in the high-rank category for the world. The Bahamas relies on tourism and offshore services but, despite having a higher GDP per capita than Barbados, spends less revenue on education and health care. Cuba, with a relatively low GDP per capita, ranks well on the scale because the Cuban government spends high percentages of GDP on education and health care. Cuba has numerous medical schools and the highest doctor to patient ratio in the world.[3] Trinidad and Tobago, a producer of oil and gas, is ranked at 54. The last Caribbean country categorized with a high HDI is Antigua-Barbuda. Antigua relies heavily on tourism and gave up growing sugar cane long ago.

Six Caribbean countries in the medium HDI category post similar scores, ranging from St Lucia with a value of 0.777 to the Dominican Republic at 0.738. People living in Grenada and the Dominican Republic have life expectancies in the sixties, while others in this Caribbean group can expect to live into their seventies. In 2006 life expectancy in Grenada rose to 71.

Haiti, ranked at 153, is the only Caribbean country in the low HDI grouping. Life expectancy in Haiti was below 50 in 2002 but was 52 in 2006. Haitian literacy levels and GDP per capita are low. Over 40 per cent of the population is under fifteen years of age, and Haiti is the least able to support a growing, young population. Haiti was first to independence (1804), but has since suffered. Twice occupied by the United States in the twentieth century, Haiti has not achieved political or economic stability.

Dependent Caribbean territories are not included in the Human Development Index. Puerto Rico and the US Virgin Islands are linked to the United States. Guadeloupe and Martinique are overseas departments of France. The Netherlands Antilles and Aruba are part of the Kingdom of the Netherlands. Britain has several small overseas territories, such as Anguilla, Montserrat, the Caymans, and Turks and Caicos Islands. Available data suggests that dependencies do well, and some do very well. For example, in the Cayman Islands life expectancy at birth is about 80 years, adult literacy is 98 per cent and GDP per capita is over $30,000 per year!

Some commentators suggest that political stability, government policies and social peace are key factors in promoting economic development, attracting investment and improving the quality of life.[4] Others think that countries with economic freedom (using factors like trade policy, government intervention and monetary policy) have produced high rates of long-term economic growth.[5] Overall, the island economies shifting to services, including tourism, are expanding, but they remain vulnerable to natural disasters, economic downturn in the northern hemisphere and changing fashions in tourism.

The Caribbean has a long history of urban development, but since the end of World War II Caribbean islands have urbanized rapidly as people moved from the countryside to towns and cities. In 1960 only about 38 per cent of people in the Caribbean lived in cities.[6] By 2006 about 65 to 70 per cent of Caribbean people lived in urban areas. As agriculture has declined coastal urban centres have grown. Some islands, such as Martinique (at 95 per cent urban), the Bahamas (89 per cent) and Puerto Rico (94 per cent), are overwhelmingly urban; others, such as St Lucia (30 per cent), St Kitts-Nevis (35 per cent) and Haiti (36 per cent), are significantly more rural (Table 3). Generally speaking, population growth rates in urban places are significantly higher than in rural areas because of in-migration.

Urbanization has increased for a number of reasons. Young adults believe there are better economic and educational opportunities in cities, if not for them then for their children. Low-paid labouring in rural areas was never attractive, and the city lights beckon, even though poor housing and high unemployment are common urban problems. Many cities, such as Kingston, Jamaica, cannot cope with the influx of people, resulting in congestion, pollution and squalid shanty towns, where crime, drugs and gangs thrive. One of the worst slums is Cité Soleil in Port-au-Prince, Haiti, where latrines are inadequate, forcing people to use open canals in the streets. Some cities, especially in the Hispanic Caribbean, have been rejuvenated in an effort to restore historic buildings and infrastructure. Santo Domingo and Havana are both UNESCO World Heritage Sites.

Shortages of adequate housing and urban infrastructure are pressing issues in most islands. Many new urban migrants first move to inner-city slums before locating to shanty towns on the periphery, where they squat on unoccupied land and erect dwellings made from corrugated iron, cardboard and plastic sheeting. Over time, residents improve self-help housing, and governments sometimes add water, sewerage and electric services. Most Caribbean countries have a primate city, which is many times larger than any other place on the island and dominates administrative and commercial activities.

Examples include Santo Domingo (2 million) in the Dominican Republic and San Juan (1 million) in Puerto Rico. In Cuba, Havana (2.2 million) remains dominant, even though Castro has focused on rural development. Socialist planning in Cuba has resulted in the growth of provincial and rural towns. Schools and health care facilities have been built in the countryside. The proportion of the total population living in primate cities can be very high. The number is over 30 per cent in San Juan, Puerto Rico, about 40 per cent in Port of Spain, Trinidad, and reaches 50 per cent in Nassau in the Bahamas. Primate cities act as political and economic centres, linking each island into the global network.

Caribbean cities have developed in much the same way as cities in the United States, with the middle classes moving out to the suburbs, leaving the Central Business District (CBD) with high-rise business buildings, a financial district and deteriorating housing and shopping. Inner-city slums and marginal shanty towns are common. The rich and poor are residentially segregated. Malls are developing on the periphery, along with some industrial parks. Capital cities of many small island states in the eastern Caribbean, such as Bridgetown (Barbados), Fort-de-France (Martinique) and Port of Spain (Trinidad), are growing rapidly, producing urban sprawl and uncontrolled expansion, which has been referred to as the urbanization of the countryside. Redevelopment of port areas is increasingly common, with work on deep-water docks to accommodate cruise ships, and attractive harbour areas to cater to tourists with duty-free shops and restaurants.

MIGRATION

The Caribbean has always been a region associated with migration and circulation, starting with the Arawaks and Caribs who moved to the islands from mainland South America. The Caribbean is an area of introduced peoples. Africans and Europeans migrated (some freely, others not) beginning in the sixteenth and seventeenth centuries, virtually eradicating the native inhabitants. Asian migrants, mainly from India and China, were added in the nineteenth century, as a wave of indentured labourers arrived. The Caribbean region has therefore one of the most diverse populations in the world, reflecting a mix of African, European and Asian ethnic heritages. Migration and mobility are facts of life for Caribbean people.

In the early twentieth century migration within the Caribbean region was common. Cane cutters moved from Jamaica and Haiti to harvest sugar in Cuba or the Dominican Republic, countries given US sugar duty preferences. Barbadians, Jamaicans and others worked on building the Panama Canal, and some stayed in Central America, where they found jobs on banana plantations. Caribbean people moved to Trinidad and the Netherlands Antilles once the oil industry was established in the 1920s. During the Depression years many islanders returned 'home' as jobs and opportunities declined. In World War II US bases on St Thomas and elsewhere acted as magnets for labour. During the war labour demands in the US led to contract workers from the Caribbean cutting cane and performing other agricultural tasks on the mainland, a practice that continues.

Since the second half of the twentieth century, migration from the region has been the dominant trend, reflecting population pressure, economic conditions and political circumstances. Some commentators talk of the circulation of Caribbean populations because people are extremely mobile, moving backwards and forwards between job opportunities (frequently overseas) and family responsibilities in the islands. Migration, often temporary, is seen as a strategy for economic survival.

Immediately after World War II, many moved to Western Europe to fill a labour vacuum. People from British-connected islands, such as Jamaica, moved to industrial areas in London and the Midlands to take jobs in transport and hospitals, which British people did not want. Although West Indians had worked in Britain during the war, the first large ship, the *Windrush*, carrying West Indian immigrants arrived at Southampton in 1948. Thousands of West Indian migrants followed. By 1962 the British Government, fearing racial and economic problems, tightened the flow of migrants from the Commonwealth (including the Caribbean, India and Pakistan) with the first of a series of Immigration Acts, which effectively reduced migration from the West Indies to the UK. As migrants have reached retirement age some have opted to return to their home island, such as Barbados, for warm winters and family contacts. As EU citizens, French West Indians have moved to France and Dutch West Indians to the Netherlands in search of jobs and education. Young migrants have sometimes found it difficult to integrate into European society, feeling alien and unwanted. On the other hand, some Europeans have chosen to live in the Caribbean.

Since the 1960s most out-migration from the Caribbean has been overwhelmingly to the United States. There are over 5 million people of Caribbean origin residing in the US. Over 2 million are from Puerto Rico, and as US citizens are not considered foreign migrants. New York City has been their favourite destination. Many return to Puerto Rico to visit family, enjoy a second home or retire. Cubans have migrated to the US over a long period of time beginning during the Ten Years War (1868–78). The Cuban patriot José Martí lived in New York for a number of years. The number of Cuban migrants climbed in the 1950s when the dictator Batista was in power, and accelerated after Castro's revolution in 1959. About 1 million Cubans, claiming political asylum, have migrated to the US since the revolution. Most Cuban migrants ('exiles') live in the Miami area, where they make up a significant political lobby in favour of continuing harsh US policies towards Cuba. Cuban migration to the US is limited to 20,000 people per year. In addition, under the 'wet foot, dry foot' rule, if Cubans arrive on dry land, they can stay. Cubans, in contrast to Haitians, are privileged. Miami, the US city with the largest foreign-born population of any in the US, has 'Little Havana' and 'Little Haiti'.

Under terms of the 1965 US Immigration and Nationality Act Caribbean migration to the US increased. Established Caribbean communities attracted migrants from all areas in the Caribbean, with the large countries of Haiti and the Dominican Republic providing significant numbers. Many families in the Dominican Republic are lucky to have a 'dominicanyork' – a relative in New York – who can help out. Jamaicans and migrants from the English-speaking Caribbean concentrate in the north-east, especially New York City. In Crown Heights, Brooklyn, a carnival has become part of Labor Day celebrations. There are small concentrations of West Indians in places like

Boston. Significant Caribbean communities exist in Canada – Haitians in Montréal; Jamaicans and people from the Anglo-Caribbean in Toronto. Circulation between islands and North America is common, for education, family visits and, sometimes, extended overstays. Since 9/11 the US has tried to enforce immigration control more stringently as part of 'homeland security'.

Migration (documented and otherwise) relieves population pressure, poverty and unemployment in the Caribbean. Emigrants send remittances to family members 'back home' that help with day-to-day living requirements. Children in Jamaica who rely on goods sent by relatives in the US are called 'barrel children' because supplies arrive in large containers. Migration is one way that Caribbean people have coped with economic deprivation in the past. Migration can result in a 'brain drain' as people with resources, skills and ambition leave the islands, but it will continue to be a response to poverty and the lack of opportunity in the future. Indeed, migration and circulation give the Caribbean its vitality and modernity. Caribbean people are frequently involved in transnational networks that include places in the Caribbean, North America and Europe. In addition, Caribbean cultures and peoples are affecting lifestyles and events in North America and Europe, contributing population, labour, ideas, innovation and energy to the native groups. Famous people in the UK of Caribbean heritage include Sir Trevor MacDonald, Dianne Abbott MP and Linford Christie OBE. In the US former Secretary of State Colin Powell (parents from Jamaica) and singer Jennifer Lopez (Puerto Rico) are well-known figures. Many second- and third-generation Caribbean communities exist outside the region.

DIVERSITY

The Caribbean is one of the most diverse regions of the world, displaying multi-ethnic and multi-linguistic societies. This makes it difficult to build a sense of regional cohesion. People have migrated from Africa, mostly West Africa, from Senegambia, the Gold Coast, the Bight of Benin, the Bight of Biafra and west-central Africa, via the slave trade.

Europeans from Spain, France, the Netherlands, Britain, Denmark, Portugal, Germany, Madeira and the Canaries, plus people from Syria and Lebanon, have contributed to the ethnic mix. Asians, especially Chinese and Indians, have enriched the cultural tapestry. The Afro-Caribbean population is the largest group. Languages spoken include Spanish (*c.* 60 per cent), English (*c.* 16 per cent), French (*c.* 22 per cent), Dutch (*c.* 2 per cent), Papiamento (in the Netherlands Antilles) and various Creole dialects, notably *Kréyol*, widely used in Haiti. Islanders display loyalty to their particular island, and some may look down on neighbouring populations. For instance, Puerto Ricans (where a large percentage of the population considers itself white) generally perceive people from the Dominican Republic as inferior, and in turn many Dominicans, who celebrate their mixed heritage, view Haitians with contempt. Loyalties can be complicated because islanders may identify with a particular ethnic group. For example, in multi-ethnic Trinidad, people might see themselves as Trinidadian, but then associate with an Afro-Caribbean heritage or East Indian background, a division built on contestation, which shows up in political affiliation. People in Tobago may see themselves as different from Trinidadians, even though they are linked together politically. Ethnicity can make feelings of nationality more complex. Similarly, ethnic and racial backgrounds can influence perceived social class.[7]

Ideas about 'race' complicate issues of identity and, despite a great deal of miscegenation, leading to a large mulatto population, degrees of whiteness continue to be associated with wealth and power. In Martinique, for example, Creole whites, known as *békés*, control much of the island's wealth. The poor and underprivileged are usually black, although attributes, such as wealth or education, can 'whiten'. In the Caribbean there are many shades of skin colour. Some commentators suggest that in recent years skin pigmentation is becoming less important as a social class indicator. This may have some relevance in small eastern Caribbean states like St Lucia and St Vincent with large black majorities and new black elites, but it may be less accurate for some of the larger countries, especially Hispanic islands, where there are generally larger percentages of people with European roots. For example, in the Dominican Republic lighter skinned people of European descent have traditionally been landowners, businessmen and professionals. The darker skinned are the urban and rural poor. This type of divide is still common in most islands, although race prejudice and discrimination are decreasing and 'inter-racial' relationships are now common. Even in Cuba, where Castro has actively pursued anti-discrimination policies, the poorest in society are usually black.

Great gulfs separate the rich from the poor in the Caribbean. Although in terms of world conditions the region (with the exception of Haiti) is relatively well off, there are still pockets of deep poverty in many islands. In Puerto Rico, it is estimated that over half the population lives in poor conditions and depends on assistance. Many Jamaicans suffer severe hardship, scratching out a living in deprived rural areas or existing in shanty towns. Malnutrition still affects poor families. Half the world's population exists on $2 or less per day, and in Jamaica it is estimated that about 13 per cent of the population lives on less than $2 a day. In Trinidad, the figure is 20 per cent, and this in an oil-producing nation.[8] Many Caribbean people live in poor housing with unreliable services, where power cuts are common.

Diversity is also apparent in forms of family structure. Various types of unions are found, ranging from 'visiting' relationships (without cohabitation) to co-residence without marriage (common law union), to legal marriage.[9] Frequently, the marriage ceremony occurs when the man can afford to buy a house, pay for a wedding and support a wife. If not, then why marry? Because of this relationship pattern, most children are born outside formal marriage into female-headed households. Many Caribbean women are highly self-reliant, frequently embedded in family and community networks that provide additional support in raising offspring. The family is a strong constituent of Caribbean society and, despite considerable migration, family links are maintained.

HEALTH CARE

Cuba, with over a quarter of the Caribbean islands' population (11.3 million), has one of the best health-care systems in the world. Infant mortality, a good indicator of health care, is an impressive 5.8 per thousand live births, just slightly higher than that in the UK (5.2), but below infant mortality rates in the US (6.6) and Puerto Rico (9.8). Since Castro came to power, a very high proportion of GDP has been directed to improving Cuban health. Emphasis is on community-based care with relatively low costs. Some Cuban doctors, because of abysmal pay, resort to driving taxis to augment income.

Health-care systems of other Caribbean nations have also improved since the 1950s. Life expectancy has increased to over 70 in most countries, except Haiti (52) and the Dominican Republic (68). Death rates, birth rates and infant mortality rates have dropped. In Haiti, the infant mortality rate is high at 80 per 1,000 live births, and in the Dominican Republic a relatively high 31 per 1,000.

Many governments, especially Barbados and the Bahamas, spend a relatively high percentage of revenue on health care, although resources can become strained with economic downturns, as in the 1980s. Emphasis has been placed on training nurses, nurses' aids and midwives. Public health initiatives have led to safer drinking water. Over 90 per cent of urban dwellers have access to improved drinking water. Infant immunization systems have been successful, and family planning programmes mean lower fertility rates as well as a decline in maternal mortality. Women in most Caribbean islands, with the exception of Puerto Rico, are eligible for paid maternity leave. For example, in Barbados and the Dominican Republic women get twelve weeks maternity leave with 100 per cent pay. In the Bahamas and Antigua-Barbuda thirteen weeks are covered at 60 per cent pay. Cuba is the most generous, allowing eighteen weeks with full pay.

Diseases such as malaria, yellow fever and tuberculosis have been tackled. Challenges to Caribbean health are now the 'diseases of the rich', such as heart disease, cancer, obesity, diabetes and hypertension. In addition, drug use, violence and HIV/AIDS threaten the health of Caribbean people.

WOMEN

Caribbean women have contributed energy and initiative to life and labour in the islands. In slavery, women of African heritage worked in the cane fields, in plantation kitchens and bedrooms, and in the markets. They produced export crops, food and children. Slave women, just as men, resisted slavery. A famous female leader in Jamaica, 'Nanny', headed the 1739 Maroon rebellion against the British. She is now a national heroine. Doña Mariana Grajales de Maceo lost nine offspring in the Cuban wars of independence and is considered the mother of Cuba.[10] Mary Seacole, the Jamaican Florence Nightingale, used her excellent nursing skills in the Crimean War (1854–6) to care for sick British soldiers in Russia. In the 1930s women emerged in labour unions of the Anglo-Caribbean, pushing for better pay and conditions. Women continue to be active in the labour movement.

Today, women play an increasing role in Caribbean economies and workforces – whether it be wage work, self-employment, part-time or informal. Caribbean women, frequently heads of household, use multiple methods to make a living for themselves and their offspring, including growing food crops for domestic consumption. They are often involved in female self-help networks. Women value economic independence and freedom of action.

Educated, middle-class women have traditionally been teachers and nurses, and increasingly find work in administrative and technical areas. Females, on average, have more years in education than males and predominate at universities and colleges. Low-wage jobs for women in factories typically involve apparel and assembly work. Wages may be low, but not as low as in China. Since NAFTA (1994) some assembly operations have moved to Mexico. Offshore data-processing services for airlines and banks, together with telemarketing, have located in the Caribbean, although this sector has not proved as promising as projected.

Most Caribbean islands have more women than men, reflecting previously high male migration.[11] Female international migration rates have increased since the 1970s, and today more women than men migrate from the Anglo-Caribbean. Women find jobs in hospitals and nursing homes in the US. Everywhere in the Caribbean life expectancy is higher for women than men. Women live to 82 in Martinique and 81 in Puerto Rico, longer than in the US, where the figure is 80 years of age. The total fertility rate (TFR), which is the average number of children born to each woman, has come down in recent years. In several countries, including Barbados, Cuba, Puerto Rico, and Trinidad and Tobago, the TFR is below 2, which is less than replacement level. Cuba has the most women in politics, with about a quarter of representatives, due to a quota system. Dame Eugenia Charles was prime minister of Dominica from 1980 to 1995. Jamaica installed its first female prime minister, Portia Simpson-Miller, in 2006.

Chapter 7

Culture

Caribbean culture is alive and kicking, combining African, Asian and European themes in a creative *mélange*. Many commentators emphasize the Creolized or transculturated nature of styles that bring diverse ingredients into the Caribbean stew, or *callaloo*. Since the end of World War II there has been an explosion of cultural creativity. In music and entertainment there are carnival, calypso, reggae and steel bands – all known globally – plus many exciting new musical styles. Island authors have written poetry, plays, essays and novels of world-class standard, producing Nobel prize winners Derek Walcott and V. S. Naipaul. Literary subject matter addresses many themes, from anti-colonialism to a history of bondage and struggle for freedom, to nationalism, to emigration, diaspora, exile and return. Local Creole dialects are used proudly as 'authentic' dialogue, expressing real-life experiences of Caribbean people. Recent literature underlines the Creole nature of Caribbean identity with all its richness, variety and informality. Fusion, a blending of multi-cultural elements and styles, describes Caribbean cultures.

Sports, especially cricket in the Anglo-Caribbean, baseball in the Hispanic islands and soccer and basketball everywhere, are played and followed with a keen interest and knowledge. In the Olympic Games Caribbean athletes compete for international recognition and island bragging rights, notably in boxing and track and field. Religious traditions are many and varied, frequently combining African and European rituals and beliefs to create new compositions known as syncretic religions. Caribbean cultural creativity includes art, ballet, dress, cuisine and drama, but this chapter focuses on music, literature, religion, sport and food.

MUSIC

The Trinidad Carnival, lasting over a month in the capital Port of Spain, is the best-known annual contemporary event in the Caribbean. Originally associated with the period before Lent, Carnival is a time of revelry, parade, music, dance, parties and playing *mas*, or masquerade. The celebration ends on 'Mardi Gras', or Fat Tuesday, and traditionally was followed by a period of fasting. Rum is central to Carnival and intrinsic to Caribbean popular culture. Carnivals are a fusion of songs, dances and styles from diverse traditions, and are now common in most islands, helping to attract tourists. Barbadians enjoy crop-over (traditionally at the end of the sugar cane harvest) and Jamaicans celebrate *jonkonu*. Carnivals have become popular outside the region, being carried to Notting Hill, London, by Caribbean migrants. A traditional carnival experience is also found in Rio de Janeiro. In the United States Carnival celebrations are associated with New Orleans, home of 'Creole' culture in the US.

Carnival songs (calypso) blend entertainment and education in a humorous style, full of social commentary. Folk wit is a crucial part of Caribbean culture, bringing people down to earth with a sense of the ridiculous. Many calypso artists, including 'The Mighty Sparrow' (Slinger Francisco 1935–), are famous inside and outside the Caribbean for lyrics, humour, wit and imagination. 'The Mighty Sparrow' has over 70 albums to his name. Harry Belafonte (1927–), although born in Harlem, New York, is of Jamaican heritage, and is probably the world's best-known calypso singer. Recognized by the *Banana Boat Song* with the 'Day O, Day O' lyric, he is an accomplished actor and social critic, outspoken in his criticism of US policy in Iraq.

Bob Marley (1945–1981), the legendary singer, guitarist and songwriter, is associated with reggae, which was born in poor black areas of Kingston, Jamaica. Reggae lyrics reflect the troubled atmosphere of the Jamaican ghetto and frequently refer to the historical background associated with slavery and oppression. Reggae is a synthesis of diverse musical styles, including Afro-Latin American forms (like the rumba) and Afro-North American jazz and rhythm and blues. Its roots are in Afro-Jamaican religious music and Jamaican *ska*, popular in the early 1960s.[1] Reggae is notable for sharp social and political commentary.

Marley was drawn to Rastafarianism after Haile Selassie, emperor of Ethiopia, visited Jamaica in 1966. Marley's music carried a spiritual message of tolerance, love and unity. The ideas of Rastafarianism (including ganja culture) are at the heart of his music. Starting in the 1960s with the 'Wailing Wailers', Marley went on to achieve international fame with such albums as *Catch a Fire* (1972) and *Burnin'* (1973) – the latter included 'Get Up, Stand Up', an appeal to the poor and marginalized in society. Many reggae songs deal with social and economic inequalities in Jamaican society.

In the political tensions of the 1970s Marley played before Michael Manley, the Jamaican prime minister, at the 'One Love Peace Concert' in Jamaica. He won a UN Peace Medal. A super-star, Marley did not survive cancer, dying in 1981. Awarded Jamaica's Order of Merit, Bob Marley received a state funeral in his home island, with politicians in attendance. His music lives on, with large royalties accruing to his foundation in Jamaica. Reggae has a worldwide, popular following, especially in Africa, and the lyrics frequently reflect a moral consciousness. Other famous reggae artists include 'Burning Spear', 'Mighty Diamonds', 'Third World' and Peter Tosh. Today reggae music, voicing issues of hunger, peace in the Middle East and global warming, attracts international audiences.

Music and dance forms are identified with particular islands, and all share an Afro-Caribbean impulse. Cuba has *danzon* and *son*. Jamaica has reggae. Calypso is linked to Trinidad, as is *soca*, a mixture of calypso and East Indian music. *Merengue*, a blend of European and African rhythms, is associated with the Dominican Republic. Artists in Martinique and Guadeloupe developed *zouk*. Puerto Rico has *salsa* ('flavour'), born in poor immigrant areas of New York and carried back to Puerto Rico and the Caribbean in general. Ricky Martin, from Puerto Rico, is an international *salsa* star, proud of his heritage and known outside the region.

Rap and hip-hop are dominant musical forms at the moment. Rap (rhythm and poetry) music emerged in US black ghettos in the 1980s, and was quickly taken up in poor black neighbourhoods in the Caribbean. Rap involves slang monologues, frequently referring to violence, sex, racism and drugs, set against pulsing rhythms and beats. It speaks the language of global youth counter-culture. Hip-hop has a musical and danceable appeal. Recent innovations in the islands include fusion music like 'chutney' in Trinidad, 'dancehall' (also known as 'raggamuffin') in Jamaica and London, and 'rapso' in the English-speaking islands. Fusion, a merging of diverse elements, is a useful way to describe Caribbean culture in general, not just in relation to musical styles. Music beats out from cars, homes, bars and buses, reflecting the vitality of Caribbean island scenes. Dance enlivens the clubs and streets everywhere. Visitors report that Cubans, young and old, spend the evenings dancing in residential streets and parks, taking advantage of an affordable form of entertainment.

LITERATURE

Anglo-Caribbean

In the early twentieth century Anglo-Caribbean writers established salons as vehicles to express Caribbean literature. H.G. De Lisser, editor of *The Gleaner* (the main newspaper in Jamaica), published *Planter's Punch* annually, starting in 1920, and Esther Chapman began the *West India Review* in 1934. In Trinidad the *Beacon Group*, associated with Alfred Mendes, C.L.R. James and Albert Gomes, produced literary journals incorporating Creole dialect in poetry and stories. There was a conscious effort to connect with popular themes and forms of speaking.[2]

Anti-colonial novels appeared in the 1930s amidst labour agitation and strikes of the Depression decade. Mendes published *Pitch Lake* (1934) and Cyril Lionel Robert James's *Minty Alley* came out in 1936. James (1901–1989), a formidable Marxist intellectual from Trinidad who started as a cricket journalist and helped Learie Constantine write his autobiography, is well known for his historical work *Black Jacobins* (1938) about the Haitian Revolution, and later *Beyond a Boundary* (1962) on cricket, politics and society. James argued that the game of cricket became so popular in the West Indies because it allowed the colonized to compete and beat the colonizers at their own game. He lived in the US from 1939 until expelled in the McCarthy era for his political views. James's work and ideas influenced the Black Power movement in the US. He was committed to the idea of West Indies Federation. In later life James campaigned for independence in the Caribbean and Africa. C.L.R. James is a significant figure in Caribbean philosophy, a champion of the oppressed masses, whose work is read and appreciated widely today.

In the 1940s a group of Caribbean artists and writers in London founded the Caribbean Artists Movement that inspired creative journals, such as *Bim*, edited in Barbados by Frank Collymore beginning in 1942. Many Caribbean writers, including Derek Walcott, contributed to *Bim*. The University College of the West Indies published *Caribbean Quarterly*, full of scholarly reviews and essays. The BBC aired *Caribbean Voices* (originally produced by the Jamaican poet Una Marson), a radio programme that acted as an outlet for the work of Caribbean writers living in the UK.

After World War II Caribbean authors produced a wide range of high-quality literature, much of it expressing frustration with migration, racism and identity issues. Two of the best-known writers, inside and outside the English-speaking Caribbean, are Derek Walcott (1930–) and V. S. Naipaul (1932–). Both men won Nobel prizes for literature – Walcott in 1992 and Naipaul in 2001. Walcott, a poet and dramatist who frequently employs calypso rhythms and Creole dialect, grew up in St Lucia, although his mother was from Dutch St Maarten. He studied in Jamaica, Trinidad and New York before teaching at Boston University. His most famous poetic piece is *Omeros* (1990). His plays include *Dream on Monkey Mountain* and the stage version of *The Odyssey* (1993). Much of his work investigates the conflict between European and West Indian cultures in a search for Caribbean identity and autonomy. In recognition of his literary accomplishments, the central square in St Lucia has been re-named in his honour.

V. S. Naipaul, born in Trinidad into a family of Hindu Indian heritage, studied at University College, Oxford, and, although well travelled, has lived most of his life in England. One of his early successful novels is *A House for Mr Biswas* (1961), based on family accounts of early experiences in Trinidad. His well-known book *The Middle Passage* appeared in 1961, and his major novel *The Mimic Men* in 1967. All together he has written more than twenty works. Much of his writing explores the problems associated with colonialism and the sense of alienation and rootlessness it breeds. Naipaul received a knighthood in 1990. Another famous author, who made her mark with *Wide Sargosso Sea* (1966), is Jean Rhys from Dominica.

Contemporary Caribbean novelists, both male and female, have been prolific. Successful writers from the Anglo-Caribbean include the Barbadians George Lamming (1927–) and Kamau Brathwaite (1930–). Lamming's *In the Castle of My Skin* is a bitter attack on colonialism and colonial education. Brathwaite read history at Cambridge University, and has published poetry and plays using Creole dialect. He is noted for contributing critical essays, history books and poetry, including his acclaimed *The Arrivants* (1973) and his doctoral dissertation (University of Sussex, 1968), published as *The Development of Creole Society in Jamaica, 1770–1820* (1971). Caryl Phillips, who left St Kitts for England when he was a baby, won the Malcolm x prize for *The Final Passage* (1985). Female authors are well represented, including Jamaica Kinkaid (born Elaine Potter Richardson in Antigua), Erna Brodber (Jamaica) and Merle Hodge (Trinidad). Exile and identity, return and disillusionment, are common themes.

The explosion of literary creativity reflects the relentless talent of Caribbean men and women. Issues of colonialism, racism, independence and identity in a tropical island setting, and in the African diaspora, have provided productive, sometimes painful, stimulants to Caribbean writers and intellectuals.

French Caribbean

In Haiti local literary work accelerated in response to US occupation between 1915 and 1934. A major focus was on Africa and black culture as the heart of Haitian identity. An early advocate of Haitian cultural nationalism was Jean Price-Mars (1876–1969). As an accomplished academic and diplomat, he is noted for *Ainsi Parla l'Oncle* (*So Spoke the Uncle*), published in 1928. Another prominent Haitian writer was the Marxist

Jacques Stephen Alexis (1922–1961), whose *Comrade General Sun* (1955) addressed the 1937 massacre of Haitians ordered by the Dominican president Trujillo. Alexis was killed by the brutal Tonton Macoutes, thugs controlled by President Duvalier.

Writers and intellectuals from Martinique and Guadeloupe are associated with the ideological movement know as *négritude* that emphasized Africa as a source of cultural identity and strength for Caribbean blacks. Aimé Césaire, born in Martinique in 1913, is a founding figure of this group who collaborated in Paris with French-speaking Africans, such as Léopold Senghor, who became president of Senegal. The journal *Etudiant Noir* (*Black Student*) published the stories and poetry of *négritude*. Césaire, a poet, dramatist and essayist, returned to Martinique as a teacher and socialist politician. His poetry is complex and difficult to comprehend. Two of his students – Frantz Fannon and Edouard Glissant – became influential writers. *Black Skins, White Masks* (1952), a psychiatric study of domination and racism, is Fannon's best-known work. Glissant continues the search for Caribbean reality, moving into the post-*négritude* period associated with *créolité* (Creolization) – the ongoing blending of cultural traits to create something new. Glissant uses the idea of Caribbean-ness to discover the many threads of identity in the Antilles. Maryse Condé from Guadeloupe has lived in Africa, Europe and the US, and is known for her novels about the African diaspora.

Hispanic Caribbean

The Hispanic Caribbean has a tradition of excellent writing, including the work of Cuban patriot José Martí and Puerto Rico's poet-politician Luis Muñoz Marín. Fernando Ortiz (1881–1969), a well-educated Cuban lawyer, professor and intellectual, wrote widely on the history, economy and culture of Cuba. He associated systems of production and types of crops (such as sugar and tobacco) with cultural and social contrasts. Ortiz acknowledged the diverse cultural contributions to Cuban history and reality, inventing the word 'transculturation' – a term in vogue today.

The contemporary Hispanic Caribbean has been involved in the Latin American boom in fiction writing. The Cuban novelist and musicologist

Alejo Carpentier (1904–1980) developed a theory of 'marvellous realism', revealing the excitement of Latin American culture and life. As a political exile in Paris between 1928 and 1939, Carpentier was influenced by the Surrealist movement. Two of his famous works are *El reino de este munde* (*The Kingdom of this World*) and *El siglo de las luces* (*Explosion in a Cathedral*). He returned to Cuba in 1959 to assist with cultural projects in Castro's regime, and later became Cuban ambassador to France.

Guillermo Cabrera Infante (1929–2005) became disaffected from Castro's regime and went into exile in London in 1965. Cabrera Infante is best known for *Tres Triste Tigres (Three Trapped Tigers)*, an experimental work that has been compared to James Joyce's *Ulysses*. Another talented author, who split with Castro's government, was Reinaldo Arenas (1943–1990). Openly gay, he committed suicide in New York, battling AIDS. José Lezama Lima (1910–1976), Cuban writer and poet, is a further figure of stature in Latin American literature.

Cuban film has been especially creative, producing high-calibre movies. Probably the most famous work is associated with Tomás Gutiérrez Alea, responsible for such films as *La Ultima Cena* (*The Last Supper*, 1976) and *Fresa y Chocolate* (*Strawberry and Chocolate*, 1993). The films of Fernando Pérez are notable, including *Clandestinos*, *Hello Hemingway* and *Madagascar*, all popular with the Cuban public.

Pedro Juan Soto wrote about experiences of Puerto Rican migrants in New York in *Spiks* (1956) and about US relations with Puerto Rico in *Usmail* (1958), both famous works. Puerto Rico's leading female author is Rosario Ferré (1938–). Her most recent novel, published in English, is *The House on the Lagoon*, a family epic depicting Puerto Rico's twentieth-century history. Other contemporary writers from the Hispanic Caribbean include Cristina García, whose *Dreaming in Cuba* (1992) is well respected.

RELIGION

Caribbean people enjoy many different religious traditions reflecting the creativity, diversity and mixing of Caribbean cultures. Most religions in the Caribbean have a Christian and/or African foundation, but have been modified to produce new creations. European religions, such as Roman Catholicism in the Latin islands and the Protestant Church of England in the Anglo areas, were introduced into the Caribbean during the colonial era, and continue to be important, particularly among elites. Hinduism and Islam, introduced with indentured labourers, are also practised, especially in Trinidad.

In the early nineteenth century Protestant groups – Methodists, Moravians and Baptists – established missions and schools in the English islands. The Spiritual Baptist faith, an Afro-Caribbean blended religion, is based in Trinidad. Newer missions, such as Jehovah's Witnesses, Seventh Day Adventists and Mormons, followed, and are still important in the region.

Santería, a neo-African religion, developed in Cuba and diffused to the Dominican Republic, Puerto Rico and elsewhere in the diaspora. Santería ('way of the saints') blends Roman Catholic ideas and practices with African (Yoruba) rituals and beliefs. It involves music, drumming, chants and animal sacrifice.

Vodou, a religious experience that evolved in the slave society of Haiti, also combines West African and Roman Catholic ideas, symbols and rituals. Powerful spirits (and Catholic saints) are believed to impact every part of life. Trance and spirit possession play an important role in vodou ceremonials. Orisha, popular in Trinidad, also has African roots.

Rastafarianism is one of the best-known Caribbean religions, associated with reggae music, wearing dreadlocks and smoking ganja (marijuana) as a spiritual act. 'Rastas' are vegetarians and oppose many aspects of modern western society, believing they are the chosen people of God. The ideas of Marcus Garvey, including blaming whites for black oppression, and the advice to look to Africa for a Messiah, helped to lay the foundations for Rastafarianism. The movement began in Jamaica in the 1930s when Haile Selassie, claiming to be an heir of King David and the Queen of Sheba, was crowned emperor of Ethiopia ('land of the blacks'). Rastas believed that the white world was evil, and that blacks would return to Africa and secure revenge against inferior whites. Today there are many subgroups around the world, but the underlying message is opposition to economic and political oppression of the poor in society.

In recent years one of the most successful religious imports to the islands is associated with a Protestant revivalist sect from the United States known as Pentacostalism. A popular branch is the Assemblies of God. Emphasis is on the Holy Spirit, speaking in tongues, singing, healing and spirit possession. The Bible is the final word in matters of faith. Charismatic leaders are important.

SPORT

Cricket

The game of cricket is played, watched and followed in the Anglo-West Indies with a passion. It is a mass spectator sport, providing heroes for the West Indian public and promoting a sense of regional identity for the English-speaking islands. Cricket highlights individual performance within a team, setting. When the West Indies Test side plays another international team, island rivalries are set aside. The accepted view is that cricket was introduced into the West Indies by British army officers early in the nineteenth century. The first cricket club was established at St Ann's, Barbados, in 1806. Similar clubs formed in Trinidad in the 1840s. In Jamaica, the Kingston Cricket Club was established in 1863.[3] Planters, merchants and colonial administrators joined the elite, white clubs. After Emancipation the game diffused to the local population and was widely played in an informal way on fields, beaches and roads, sometimes with improvised equipment, such as small coconuts!

By the second half of the nineteenth century cricket was established at grammar schools in the region, like Harrison College, Barbados and Queen's Royal College, Trinidad. Clubs, usually organized on ethnic or class basis, were emerging, and village players showed good skills. One of the best-known black clubs was the Shannon Cricket Club in Trinidad, where the famous Constantines (father and son) played.

The sons of British administrators in the West Indies were sometimes taught cricket by locals who worked at the houses and grounds. For example, Pelham Warner (1873–1963), born in Trinidad as the son of the Chief Secretary, remembered being bowled to by Killebree, who did jobs around the house, apparently including cricket coaching! After schooling in Trinidad, Warner attended Harrison College, Barbados, which had at least three cricket teams. He went on to play for Oxford University, Middlesex and England. When Warner returned to Trinidad in 1896–7 with Lord Hawke's team to tour the West Indies a number of locals reminded him they had taught him his cricket.[4] At elite, white clubs black cricketers were sometimes hired as groundskeepers and bowled to members in the nets.

The first inter-regional cricket match was played between Barbados and British Guyana in 1865, and other regional fixtures followed.[5] The first English team toured the West Indies in 1895, and five years later, in 1900, a West Indian team, including L. S. Constantine (father of Lord Learie Constantine), played in England, where Constantine senior made a century at Lords. By the 1920s and '30s the West Indians were involved in cricket tours in England, India and Australia, gaining Test status in 1928.

During the years of colonial rule race was a factor in selecting the West Indies team, with the assumption that the captain would be white, just as in England it was assumed that the captain would be an amateur. Many felt that the young George Hedley should have been selected for the 1928 tour of England after he made a double century for Jamaica against Lord Tennyson's touring side in 1927. He did make his Test debut at Bridgetown in 1930, and scored a century. On tours to England in 1933 and 1939 Hedley scored well, but had the disadvantage of frequently carrying the West Indian batting. Even so his average exceeded 60.

The ebullient Learie Constantine was the star West Indian all-rounder between the wars who played in the Lancashire leagues. At the end of his cricketing career he read law, becoming a barrister in 1954. He went on to a distinguished political life, working for the independence of Trinidad and becoming High Commissioner for Trinidad and Tobago in Britain from 1962 to 1964. Constantine spoke out about discrimination in cricket, believing selection should be based on merit, not race or class. He was convinced that, in order for the West Indies to show its full potential, the captain should be black. In life he challenged racism, winning a legal case against a London hotel that discriminated against him and his family in 1943.

World War II interrupted Test cricket but inter-island cricket was played and new stars emerged. When an MCC team toured the islands early in 1948 it did not win a match. In 1950 the West Indies cricket team won three out of four Test matches in England, giving West Indians pride in beating the colonial power. Some commentators have suggested that West Indian cricket was reconstructed as a form of cultural resistance.[6] In the 1950 Test matches three Barbadian batsmen – 'the three Ws' of Walcott, Weekes and Worrell – helped the West Indies to victory. So too did the famous spinners, 'those two little pals of mine / Ramadhin and Valentine', as Lord Kitchener's catchy calypso couplet reminds us.

In 1955 Australia was defeated by the West Indies when the Barbadian Garfield Sobers made his mark. Two years later, Sobers hit 365 runs in the test match against Pakistan, beating Sir Len Hutton's record. Sobers's record has since been passed by the Trinidadian Brian Lara. Sobers, a powerful batsman, successful bowler, accomplished fielder and astute captain (1968–74), is the best all-round cricket player in the history of the game. In 1960 Frank Worrell, a Barbadian, became the first black to captain the West Indies side on a tour to Australia, a tour known as the 'Calypso Summer'. Worrell had been asked twice previously to be captain, but insisted on finishing a degree at Manchester University before taking on the role. His calm leadership was an important factor in the West Indies winning the 1963 Tests in England by three matches to one. Worrell's captaincy underlined the fact the blacks could lead effectively. Both Worrell and Sobers were knighted. Frank Worrell, who died of leukaemia in 1967, just 42 years old, is buried in Barbados. He received a memorial service at Westminster Abbey, the first sportsman to be so honoured.

During the 1970s and '80s West Indian teams were dominant on the international circuit. Remarkable players included Wes Hall, Malcolm Marshall, Clive Lloyd and Vivian Richards. In 1984 the West Indies won all five Tests against England under Lloyd's leadership. Again in 1985–6 in the West Indies, all five test matches against England were West Indian victories, this time with Richards as captain. The 1990s and beyond have not been so kind to the West Indies, despite the huge talent of Brian Lara, who scored a brilliant 375 runs in the 1994 Test in Antigua. West Indies cricket is the most popular regional institution in the Anglo-

Caribbean, acting as a source of pride, unity and competition. Test selectors try to get a balanced team representing different West Indian islands. Cricket is included on CARICOM agendas.

The importance of cricket in Anglo-West Indian life is reflected in the number of cricketing knights produced in the region. West Indian prime ministers have recommended many cricketers for honours, including Sir Frank Worrell, Sir Garfield Sobers, Sir Clyde Walcott (former Chair of the International Cricket Council) and Sir Vivian Richards. A knighthood for Lara is unlikely because Trinidad is a republic and does not recognize Queen Elizabeth as head of state.

Attention will be focused on the Caribbean when the 2007 World Cup is played in the West Indian islands of Antigua, Barbados, Grenada, Jamaica, St Lucia, St Kitts and Trinidad. Teams from Australia, Bangladesh, Bermuda, Canada, England, India, Ireland, the Netherlands, New Zealand, Pakistan, Scotland, South Africa, Sri Lanka and Zimbabwe will compete in the World Cup. Fifty-one matches will be played, with the final scheduled for Barbados. Several island governments hurry to complete facilities, including the Challenor Stand at Kensington Oval in Barbados, a stand that commemorates a prosperous Barbadian who went on cricket tours to England in the early 1900s. In 1923 George Challenor hit eight hundreds and over 1,500 runs, averaging more than 50. The World Cup will be a sporting and commercial extravaganza, complete with merchandise and a mascot called *Mello*.

Baseball

Baseball is the major team sport in the Hispanic Caribbean, played professionally in Cuba, the Dominican Republic and Puerto Rico. The first organized baseball game was played in Cuba in 1874, and professional leagues opened in that island in 1878. Cubans spread the game to the Dominican Republic where the first team – *Tigers del Licey* (The Tigers) – was founded in 1907. In the 1920s baseball competitions involved the Dominican Republic, Cuba, Puerto Rico and the US. Caribbean sportsmen began playing in US leagues despite issues associated with segregation. In the 1920s Cuban pitcher Adolfo Luque played for the Cincinnati Reds. The great Roberto Clemente from Puerto Rico was successful for the Pittsburgh Pirates between 1955 and the early 1970s, earning a place in the baseball Hall of Fame.

Fidel Castro, a good pitcher in his youth, tried to de-emphasize baseball when he gained power in Cuba because of its associations with the United States. Popular enthusiasm prevailed and today baseball is big in Cuba. The Cubans have won three of the last four Olympic gold medals for baseball. The US occupation of the Dominican Republic (1916–24) strengthened baseball in that country. In the 1970s North American major league clubs started to establish baseball academies in the Dominican Republic to train young players for a move to the mainland. Some authors have compared these academies to multinational corporations, like the sugar giant Gulf and Western, because they seek raw talent and finish it for export to the North American market.[7] Today the Dominican Republic is a significant exporter of baseball talent to the major and minor leagues in the US. The sugar mill town of San Pedro de Macoris, near Santo Domingo, is famous for producing high-quality players. Everywhere you go in the Dominican Republic, even the poorest areas, you see baseball fields and parks.

Currently, many North American major league teams, including the Toronto Blue Jays and the Los Angeles Dodgers, have year-round training camps in the Dominican Republic. Boys usually aged seventeen or eighteen 'try out' and, if selected, attend camps where they are housed, fed, coached and paid. Those showing extreme promise go into the minor leagues in the US, hoping to be promoted to the majors. Several Dominican baseball stars, including Sammy Sosa, Jose Rijo and Alex Rodriguez, have been very successful in US major leagues.

In the spring of 2006 the inaugural World Baseball Classic saw fourteen countries (including Canada, Japan, Venezuela, Panama and Mexico) compete for the championship. Puerto Rico sent its own team, as did the talented Dominican Republic. Cuba was initially excluded from the competition because the Bush administration did not want Castro to gain financially. After Cuban officials offered to donate profits to victims of Hurricane Katrina, Cuba was cleared to play. Japan beat Cuba in the final.

The Olympic Games

Participation in the Olympic Games has political and nationalistic overtones, offering Caribbean nations an opportunity to shine in the international arena. Given the relatively small size of island populations and economies, Caribbean athletes have performed well in the Games, especially in boxing and track and field. Cuba has excelled in boxing with a total of at least 30 Olympic gold medals. Teófilo Stevenson (1952–) won three heavyweight golds for Cuba in 1972, 1976 and 1980.

Since 1952 and 'commonwealth status' Puerto Rico has been able to compete in the Olympics as a separate 'nation', giving Puerto Ricans a sense of national pride and a chance to wave the Puerto Rican flag. Six of Puerto Rico's Olympic medals have been in boxing, three won by Félix 'Tito' Trinidad.[8] In the boxing world John Ruiz, a US Latino with a Puerto Rican background, won the World Boxing Association heavyweight title in 2001, dispelling the idea that Latin Americans could not win in this division. In Olympic competition, Puerto Ricans have the option of representing the US, as Gigi Fernández did in tennis doubles at the 1992 Barcelona Olympics, or Puerto Rico. Even though Fernández won the gold medal the victory was tainted in Puerto Rico because she did not represent her home island.

Many Caribbean Olympic athletes are notable. Arthur Wint of Jamaica won gold and silver in each of the London (1948) and Helsinki (1952) Games. Trinidad's Hasley Crawford won the gold medal in the 100-metre dash in Montréal (1976). But of all the Caribbean athletes, Merlene Ottey's sprinting career is the most remarkable. Born in Jamaica and educated at the University of Nebraska, Ottey competed in seven Olympic Games, six for her native Jamaica and most recently in 2004 (Athens) for Slovenia. She has won a total of eight medals, the first in Moscow (1980), the last, twenty years later, in Sydney.

Soccer is popular in the entire Caribbean as it is in Latin America in general. Jamaica made it to the World Cup in 1998. Trinidad qualified for the 2006 World Cup after beating Bahrain. There were lots of cheers for the 'soca warriors' in Trinidad.

Basketball is played across the Caribbean and is a growing part of youth culture. Televised basketball games from the US have helped to spread the popularity of the sport. In the Anglo-Caribbean islands, such as Barbados and Trinidad and Tobago, basketball is played informally by young black males for entertainment. Basketball courts offer a meeting place and social space. Voluntary associations organize leagues and run competitive fixtures.

FOOD

In recent years local Caribbean food has become popular in island hotels and restaurants. Red snapper, king fish and flying fish, caught in Caribbean waters, are found on menus. Locally grown fruits, such as mango, coconut, guava and papaya, are popular. 'Jerked' meats and curried goat can be ordered. In North American and European cities Caribbean restaurants and takeaways have opened, patronized by customers from all over the world. From Trinidad to Toronto, San Juan to San Francisco, Nevis to Notting Hill and Barbados to Boston, Caribbean cuisine has arrived – part of gastronomic globalization.

Caribbean food reflects a multi-cultural history, bringing together foods and recipes from the Americas, Africa, Europe and Asia. The first migrants to the region, the Amerindians (Arawak, Taino and Carib) from South America, ate a diet rich in fish and seafood, and grew cassava (manioc), a starchy root crop, needing careful processing to remove poisons. They also raised sweet potatoes and arrowroot. Cassava remains an important crop in the islands and in West Africa, introduced there by slave traders. The root will keep in the ground for up to three years. It is made into flour/meal and bread, and can be boiled and eaten as a vegetable, as can the green leaves. Tapioca, a refined starch common outside the region, is made from cassava.

European colonists, beginning with the Spanish, brought fruits, such as citrus, a wide range of vegetables (including onions) and meats. Spaniards introduced pigs, cattle, goats and sheep. A number of crops, including the potato, were introduced into Caribbean cooking from mainland Latin America. Rice and beans or peas is a common dish in the Caribbean. Sugar and bananas were brought from the Old World and became important in the region as plantation crops. Sugar cane, originally domesticated in New Guinea, was introduced by Christopher Columbus on his second voyage in 1493. Grown by enslaved Africans, sugar cane explains why many islands have large Afro-Caribbean populations. Saltfish, usually cod, an important source of protein for labourers, was imported from North Atlantic waters and continues to be popular in many islands. Breadfruit, transplanted to the Caribbean by Captain Bligh from Tahiti, remains part of Caribbean diets. The large fruit, grown on tall trees, can be boiled or fried much like potatoes. Bananas (plantains), eaten both raw and cooked, are enjoyed throughout the region. Plantains can be boiled, fried, roasted and baked. In the Spanish-speaking Caribbean fried plantains, *tostones*, are popular.

Foods typically associated with Caribbean cuisine were introduced from Africa. These include okra or gumbo (pods of the mallow family eaten as a vegetable), ackee (a fruit used as a vegetable with pulp that looks like scrambled eggs), yams and *callaloo* (a green, leafy crop similar to spinach). *Callaloo* is also the name of a thick soup/stew, rich in greens (such as taro/dasheen and malango) that includes vegetables and meats, flavoured with garlic, herbs and spices. Coconut milk is often used. Pepper pot is another traditional stew that originated in Guyana, made with meats, fish and vegetables at hand, and simmered for hours. A crucial ingredient is cassareep, syrup made from cassava, brown sugar and spices, which acts as a preservative. Pepper pot can be kept without refrigeration if boiled daily.

Indentured workers from the Indian sub-continent and China introduced curries, spices and other ingredients, favouring rice as a staple. East Indians brought *rotis*, flour patties with a filling of curried meat and potatoes – a spicy version of Cornish pasties. Caribbean cuisine is a mixture (dare one say a melting pot?) of American, European, African and Asian food mores. Many dishes are spicy and extra seasoning is provided from the bottles of hot sauce found on every Caribbean table. US fast food chains such as McDonald's, Kentucky Fried Chicken and Taco Bell are widespread, except in Cuba. Street vendors selling local dishes like jerked chicken or patties (*empanadas*) are everywhere.

Most islands have a special dish. In the Dominican Republic *sancocho* is a favourite thick stew, served with rice and avocado. In Puerto Rico *mondongo*, a tripe stew, is said to be good for hangovers. Cubans eat *ajiaco*, containing meats, sweet potatoes, green plantain and hot peppers. Jamaicans claim salt fish and ackee as a national dish, although jerked pork and chicken are popular. Jerked meats are marinated in a mixture of spices, including allspice, before being cooked over an open fire, barbecue style. Every cook has a special marinade. Curried goat and meat patties are also common in Jamaica. Several goat recipes have developed in the French Antilles. Trinidad's fast-food dish, known as *doubles*, is made from fried dough filled with curried chickpeas and served with mango or pepper sauce. In Barbados flying fish and *cou cou* (cornmeal and okra, probably linked to West African *foo foo*) are popular local dishes. Salted codfish fritters are eaten in Guadeloupe.

Food is washed down with a range of drinks including tropical fruit juices, coffee and locally produced beers, such as Red Stripe in Jamaica, Carib in Trinidad, Stingray in the Caymans, Kalik in the Bahamas and Banks in Barbados. Of course, every island has its favourite rum, including Mount Gay in Barbados, Bacardi in Puerto Rico and Myers in Jamaica.

There is fear that, because of globalization and Americanization, the Caribbean will lose some of its local cultural wealth. Orlando Patterson, the well-respected Jamaican Professor of Sociology at Harvard University, disputes this view, believing that cultures are forever interacting and cross-fertilizing.[9] Mass migration and circulation of Caribbean people, and modern technologies of communication and travel, encourage the creation of dynamic cultural forms in music, dance, literature, art and cuisine. The result will be continuing creativity in the Caribbean and around the Atlantic world.

Chapter 8

Problems and Prospects in the Twenty-first Century

Since the end of World War II in 1945, the Caribbean islands have changed dramatically. Politically, against a previous background of conquest and competing colonialism, the region has evolved a variety of political systems. Dictatorship, democracy, socialism and communism have all been tried. Today, with the exception of Haiti, where democracy fails to root, and Cuba, where communism rules, liberal democracies are the dominant political style. In the independent Anglo-Caribbean islands there is debate about constitutional change, including replacing the British sovereign as head of state and abolishing legal appeals to the Privy Council in London. A Caribbean Court of Justice, based in Trinidad, is now established.

Attachment to colonial powers persists in the French and Dutch Antilles, in several small British-connected islands and in Puerto Rico, but it is a voluntary relationship with a large amount of self-government. The United States is hegemonic in the region, while providing aid, markets and a destination for migrants. The influence of the US is everywhere, from merchandise and shopping malls, to cell phones, movies, the media and McDonald's. The US has intervened directly in the region, has manipulated political events and has financial and economic oversight through the World Bank and International Monetary Fund.

The list of US Caribbean interventions is long, starting with the Spanish-American War (1898) and then the decision to support a

Panamanian breakaway from Colombia in 1903, so that the US could complete the Panama Canal, linking the Caribbean to the Pacific in 1914. During World War I the US invaded Veracruz on the Caribbean coast of Mexico, and intervened in the Dominican Republic (1916–24) and Haiti (1915–34). The Danish Caribbean islands were purchased in 1917 to become the US Virgin Islands.

In the last half-century the US has interfered in the Dominican Republic (1965), landed troops in Grenada (1983), Panama (1989) and Haiti (1994), and consistently worked, since 1959, to disrupt Cuban relations and trade with Caribbean neighbours, trade that would have strengthened inter-Caribbean commercial links. The lengths to which the United States Government is prepared to go was signalled in March 2006, when a group of Cuban officials and US oilmen met in a Mexico City Sheraton hotel to discuss the possibilities of US oil companies working to develop Cuban petroleum resources. The US Treasury told the Sheraton that the gathering was against US law. The hotel evicted the Cuban delegation. The mayor of Mexico City considered the foreign interference intolerable.

Caribbean economies have changed markedly since World War II, shifting from export agriculture (mostly sugar and bananas) to service sector dominance. Tourism is now the major generator of foreign exchange. The challenge is to develop sustainable tourism, while promoting stewardship of the environment. Industry and manufacturing have been added in some islands, notably the Greater Antilles and Trinidad. Economic competition comes from low-wage Asian countries. Offshore services, including banking, insurance and data processing, contribute to the economic mix.

Most Caribbean islands (except Cuba) are heavily dependent on the US for imports, export markets and tourists. All have significant trade deficits with the US. Many face a substantial debt problem. The US continues a trade embargo against Cuba, and tries to isolate the island from the international community. Yet Cuba, with its resources and population, is the natural centre for Caribbean economic interaction. US policy towards Cuba, now largely driven by the need to please the Cuban exile population in Florida, punishes the whole Caribbean region economically by restricting island trade with Cuba. One plus of

Cuba's economic isolation is that international hotel chains and property developers with US interests have stayed away from Havana. Old Havana, a World Heritage Site, retains many historic neighbourhoods.

Although large gulfs continue to separate the haves and have-nots in Caribbean societies, most people have experienced significant improvement in quality of life. Social indicators, such as life expectancy, infant mortality and literacy rates, have improved considerably since 1945. Governments have invested in human capital, including education and health care, and overall (with the exception of Haiti) the results are positive, although too many remain poor and unemployed. A future issue will involve caring for ageing populations.

The Caribbean islands face challenges in the globalizing atmosphere of the twenty-first century if human development is to be maintained and improved. The environment is at the heart of the tourist industry and needs to be managed and protected. Environmental threats impinge on coastal and forest ecosystems. Natural hazards, such as hurricanes and flooding, are expected every year. Volcanic eruptions and earthquakes come unexpectedly. Humans continue to degrade the environment with pollution from agriculture, urban populations and tourists. Common issues across the region include hurricane damage, flooding, drought, soil erosion, coral reef damage, deforestation and pollution of coastal waters.

Tourists are a mixed blessing. They generate jobs and revenue but increase pollution and stress the environment. Cruise ships discharge effluent into the sea. Coral reefs and fish populations are in danger. Hotel and resort construction can be detrimental to beaches and landscapes. Environmental oversight involves maintaining a balance between protection of land, sea and species, while creating economic development, jobs and incomes. Global warming and the resultant rise in sea level will impact all islands, for the major towns and cities are in coastal locations.

Today, most Caribbean governments and societies are attuned to environmental issues, even if finances are not always available and organization is sometimes lacking. Many governments are party to international treaties on biodiversity, climate change, marine dumping, ozone-layer protection and the like. National parks have been set aside with over 600 protected areas in the region.[1] Some commentators talk of a recent 'boom' in conservation projects, involving parks and reserves, the development of humanized landscapes and urban environmental protection.[2] Many advocates encourage cooperation between agencies like the World Bank and United Nations, Caribbean governments, NGOs and local communities to achieve best success in preserving environments.

If environmental concerns are pressing, economic issues top the agenda of Caribbean people and politicians. Can island economies compete in the global marketplace? How will jobs and opportunities be increased? How can the region attract investment and develop infrastructure? How can small, open economies compete in a globalizing system where giant corporations and countries have many advantages?

Globalization encourages economic restructuring. Will the Caribbean remain marginalized, or can certain sectors or places capitalize on competition and comparative advantage to benefit from globalization? Some commentators are pessimistic, thinking that core countries, and those with strategic resources, will prosper, while economic development in areas like the Caribbean will suffer. Others believe that global competition and market forces will produce benefits for all.

It is common to suggest that the Caribbean, given a history of imported labour, production for export markets and outside control, has been globalized for several hundred years. In reality, the islands were tightly controlled European overseas estates attached to defined markets. Modern globalization of the 'Information Age' is new and different. It involves a revolution in communications technology. The expansion of modern technology is imperative if the Caribbean is to be competitive in the knowledge-based economy. There is room for improvement in education, especially at the tertiary level. Adult illiteracy is high in some countries, notably Jamaica, the Dominican Republic and Haiti, and a relatively small percentage of the population goes on to higher education. But there are exceptions, such as Barbados, where adult literacy is comparable to Western European countries. Schooling at elementary and secondary level is available to all, and a growing percentage of the population experiences higher education at the University of the West Indies' Cave Hill campus, the Community College or the Polytechnic. Puerto Rico has numerous universities and colleges, in addition to the University of Puerto Rico, near San Juan, with over 60,000 students, although the adult literacy rate is below that of Barbados and Cuba.

Today, Caribbean economies rely on the service sector, with tourism dominant. Agriculture is declining in output and employment, as trade preferences to Europe and the US are reduced. But modern economies are service-sector economies, and tourism will continue to rule. The challenge is to out-perform competitive destinations. The tourist industry needs to be linked to other sectors of the economy, such as hotel refitting and furniture making. Far more food could be grown in Caribbean islands and used to supply hotels and restaurants. There is an opportunity for island governments to encourage farming and develop marketing mechanisms to see that good, fresh, locally grown produce is available to islanders and visitors.

The Caribbean would benefit from improved communications and transportation both inside and outside the region. Inter-island air travel is notoriously difficult with routes often going through Miami, reflecting US dominance of the airline industry. Flights from Jamaica to Haiti, for example, go via Miami, adding time, miles and cost. Several regional airlines, such as Air Jamaica, BWIA and LIAT, survive, but are financially vulnerable, as are many large US airlines.

Institutions of economic cooperation are in place but impediments to inter-island trade and movement of labour and capital continue. Talks concerning a Caribbean single market are on hold. CARICOM (the Caribbean Common Market and Community) could be strengthened and deepened. The Association of Caribbean States (ACS), with headquarters in Port of Spain, Trinidad, is actively pursuing inter-regional cooperation. The ACS is composed of the Caribbean islands (including Cuba), plus the circum-Caribbean countries of Mexico, Venezuela, Colombia and Central America. The current ACS focus is on trade, transport, sustainable tourism and response to natural disasters, all areas that warrant attention. The Caribbean is beginning to realize that regional cooperation, not competition, can help economic development and improve the quality of life for Caribbean people.

If the Free Trade Area of the Americas (FTAA) moves forward, Caribbean countries will need initial protections and assistance to survive in competition with larger economies. Structural adjustment funds to help the economic development of small economies should be available, as they are in the EU.

Social problems afflict most islands. Illegal activities involving drugs and money laundering are common. The Caribbean is on the route of cocaine and heroine traffickers from South America. Crime is globalized. Unemployment, gangs and violence are major issues. Rates of HIV/AIDS are high in some islands, notably Haiti.

Migration (documented and undocumented) will remain a strategy for Caribbean people, and remittances will continue to help families. Caribbean people, cultures, music, festivities, food and values have travelled around the Atlantic world, enriching societies in the Americas and Europe. Cultural creativity, adaptability and resilience will continue to be strengths of Caribbean societies.

The Caribbean islands have advantages in connecting to the wider world. In a globalizing environment Caribbean diversity is an asset. The Hispanic Caribbean (and approximately 60 per cent of Caribbean islanders are Spanish-speaking) has links and affinities with mainland Latin America and the Iberian Peninsula. The Dominican Republic has recently been included in the Central American Free Trade Agreement (CAFTA) that connects Central American economies into markets and investment opportunities in the US. The Dominican Republic has simultaneously attracted capital and tourists from Western Europe, plus the United Arab Emirates has invested in Dominican port facilities.

The French and Dutch Antilles enjoy strong connections to European countries, and retain membership in the European Union. They are eligible for EU concessions and subsidies, and citizens have legal migration destinations in Europe. The Anglo-Caribbean nations and overseas territories are in the Commonwealth, which also includes such multicultural societies as South Africa, Canada, Nigeria and India.

International relationships are evident in the sporting arena, where in 2006 islands of the Hispanic Caribbean – Cuba, the Dominican Republic and Puerto Rico – played in the inaugural World Baseball Classic against mainland Latin teams, such as Venezuela and Mexico, plus Japan, South Korea and the US. Japan beat Cuba in the final. In 2007 the Anglo-Caribbean islands host the Cricket World Cup, a sporting festival that sees teams from as far away as Australia and South Africa visiting the Caribbean. Journalists and television networks from around the world will cover matches, and thousands will visit the islands as spectators. Some will take the opportunity to travel to neighbouring islands with a French, Spanish or Dutch heritage. The entire Caribbean will become better known as a result of hosting a major sporting event. Most visitors will be attracted to the cultural diversity and vitality of the Caribbean region.

References

Introducing the Contemporary Caribbean

1 Gary S. Elbow, 'Regional Cooperation in the Caribbean: The Association of Caribbean States', *Journal of Geography*, 96 (1996), pp. 13–22.
2 B. W. Blouet and O. M. Blouet, eds, *Latin America and the Caribbean: A Systematic and Regional Survey*, 5th edn (New York, 2006).

Chapter 1: Geographical Setting and Environment

1 David Watts, *The West Indies: Patterns of Development, Culture and Environmental Change since 1492* (Cambridge, 1987).
2 www.joyousjam.com/jamaicashurricanehistory, accessed 12 March 2006, author's transcription.
3 J. Molinelli, 'Earthquake Vulnerability Study for the Metropolitan Area of San Juan, Puerto Rico', in D. Barker, ed., *Proceedings of a Meeting of Experts on Hazard Mapping in the Caribbean* (Mona, Jamaica, 1989), pp. 71–86.
4 R. E. Robertson et al., 'Volcano Surveillance and Hazard Mitigation in the Eastern Caribbean', *Caribbean Geography*, 8 (1997), pp. 1–17.
5 C. Bridenbaugh and R. Bridenbaugh, *No Peace Beyond the Line: The English in the Caribbean, 1624–1690* (New York, 1972).
6 M. Moreno Fraginals, *Between Slavery and Free Labor: The Spanish-Speaking Caribbean in the Nineteenth Century* (Baltimore, MD, 1985).
7 Bonham C. Richardson, *The Caribbean in the Wider World, 1492–1992* (Cambridge, 1992).
8 Robert B. Potter et al., *The Contemporary Caribbean* (Harlow, Essex, 2004).
9 Ibid.
10 J. Diamond, *Collapse: How Societies Choose to Fail or Succeed* (New York, 2005).
11 Ibid.

Chapter 2: History to 1945

1 Bartolomé de las Casas, *The Devastation of the Indies: A Brief Account*, trans. Herma Briffault (Baltimore, MD, 1992).
2 J. H. Parry and P. Sherlock with A. P. Maingot, *A Short History of the West Indies*, 4th edn (London, 1987).
3 Philip D. Curtin, *The Atlantic Slave Trade: A Census* (Madison, WI, 1969).
4 Eric Williams, *Capitalism and Slavery* (1944) (Chapel Hill, NC, 1994).
5 Robert West and J. P. Augelli, *Middle America: Its Lands and People*, 3rd edn (Englewood Cliffs, NJ, 1989).
6 Bonham C. Richardson, *The Caribbean in the Wider World, 1492–1992* (Cambridge, 1992).
7 Selwyn Carrington, *The Sugar Industry and the Abolition of the Slave Trade, 1775–1810* (Gainesville, FL, 2002).
8 Bryan Edwards, *An Historical Survey of the French Colony in the Island of St Domingo* (London, 1797).
9 David Brion Davis, 'Impact of the French and Haitian Revolutions', in David P. Geggus, ed., *The Impact of the Haitian Revolution in the Atlantic World* (Columbia, SC, 2001).
10 Seymour Drescher, *Econocide: British Slavery in the Era of Abolition* (Pittsburgh, PA, 1977).
11 Richardson, *The Caribbean in the Wider World*, and Louis A. Pérez, Jr, *Cuba: Between Reform and Revolution*, 3rd edn (New York and Oxford, 2006).
12 Richardson, *The Caribbean in the Wider World*, p. 86.
13 Thomas J. D'Agostino, 'Caribbean Politics', in Richard S. Hillman and Thomas J. D'Agostino, eds, *Understanding the Contemporary Caribbean* (Boulder, CO, 2003).
14 Howard Johnson, 'The British Caribbean from Demobilization to Constitutional Decolonization', in Judith M. Brown and W. Roger Louis, *The Oxford History of the British Empire: The Twentieth Century* (Oxford, 1999).
15 B. R. Mitchell, *International Historical Statistics: The Americas, 1750–2000*, 5th edn (London, 2003).

Chapter 3: Caribbean Foreign Relations since 1945

1 James Ferguson, *The Story of the Caribbean People* (Kingston, Jamaica, 1998).
2 Louis A. Pérez, Jr, *Cuba: Between Reform and Revolution*, 3rd edn (New York and Oxford, 2006).
3 J.H. Parry and P. Sherlock with A.P. Maingot, *A Short History of the West Indies*, 4th edn (London, 1987).
4 Pérez, *Cuba*, p. 252.

5 Ferguson, *The Story of the Caribbean People.*
6 Ibid.
7 W. Roger Louis, 'The Dissolution of the British Empire', in Judith M. Brown and W. Roger Louis, eds, *The Oxford History of the British Empire: The Twentieth Century* (Oxford, 1999).
8 Gary Elbow, 'The Caribbean: Why Do We Care?', paper presented at the Annual Meeting, National Council for Geographic Education, Birmingham, AL, 15 October 2005.

Chapter 4: Politics since World War II

1 James Ferguson, *The Story of the Caribbean People* (Kingston, Jamaica, 1998).
2 Thomas J. D'Agostino, 'Caribbean Politics', in Richard S. Hillman and Thomas J. D'Agostino, eds, *Understanding the Contemporary Caribbean* (Boulder, CO, 2003).
3 Robert B. Potter et al., *The Contemporary Caribbean* (Harlow, Essex, 2004), chapter 12.
4 Ibid., p. 461.
5 B. Riddell, 'A Tale of Contestation, Disciples and Damned: The Lessons of the Spread of Globalization into Trinidad and Tobago', *Environment and Planning*, 35 (2003), pp. 659–78.

Chapter 5: Economies

1 B. R. Mitchell, *International Historical Statistics: The Americas, 1750–2000* (New York, 2003).
2 Robert West and J. P. Augelli, *Middle America: Its Lands and People* (Englewood Cliffs, NJ, 1966), p. 189.
3 Robert B. Potter et al., *The Contemporary Caribbean* (Harlow, Essex, 2004), chapter 3.
4 Anthony P. Maingot, 'Rum, Revolution and Globalization: Past, Present and Future of a Caribbean Product', in Franklin W. Knight and Teresita Martínez-Vergne, eds, *Contemporary Caribbean Cultures and Societies in a Global Context* (Chapel Hill, NC, 2005). See also Frederick H. Smith, *Caribbean Rum: A Social and Economic History* (Gainesville, FL, 2005).
5 www.wto.org.
6 Ibid.
7 www.iadb.org.
8 H. Michael Erisman, 'International Relations', in Richard S. Hillman and Thomas J. D'Agostino, eds, *Understanding the Contemporary Caribbean* (Boulder, CO, 2003).

9 Thomas Klak, 'Globalization, Neoliberalism and Economic Change in Central America and the Caribbean', in Robert Gwynne and C. Kay, eds, *Latin America Transformed: Globalization and Modernity*, 2nd edn (London, 2004).
10 Potter et al., *The Contemporary Caribbean*, chapter 8.

Chapter 6: People and Society

1 B.R. Mitchell, *International Historical Statistics: The Americas, 1750–2000* (New York, 2003).
2 A. Downes, 'Economic Growth and Development in Barbados during the Twentieth Century', *Integration and Trade Journal*, 15 (2001), pp. 145–76.
3 Robert B. Potter et al., *The Contemporary Caribbean* (Harlow, Essex, 2004), chapter 5.
4 Ronald Ramkissoon, 'Explaining Differences in Economic Performance in Caribbean Economies' and 'Small Caribbean Economies: What Are We Doing Wrong?', www.cid.harvard.
5 Marc Miles, Edwin Feulner and Mary O'Grady, 2005 Index of Economic Freedom, www.Heritage.org.
6 Potter et al., *The Contemporary Caribbean*, chapter 7.
7 David Baranov and Kevin A. Yelvington, 'Race, Class, and Nationality', in Richard S. Hillman and Thomas D'Agostino, eds, *Understanding the Contemporary Caribbean* (Boulder, CO, 2003).
8 Population Reference Bureau, *Population Data Sheet* (Washington, DC, 2005).
9 Baranov and Yelvington, 'Race', in *Understanding the Contemporary Caribbean*, chapter 8.
10 A. Lynn Bolles, 'Women and Development', in *Understanding the Contemporary Caribbean*, chapter 9.
11 Janet Henshall Momsen, 'Women and Development in the Caribbean', in B. W. Blouet and O. M. Blouet, eds, *Latin America and the Caribbean: A Systematic and Regional Survey* (New York, 2006).

Chapter 7: Culture

1 Jorge L. Giovanetti, 'Jamaican Reggae and the Articulation of Social and Historical Consciousness in Musical Discourse', in Franklin W. Knight and Teresita Martínez-Vergne, eds, *Contemporary Caribbean Cultures and Societies in a Global Context* (Chapel Hill, NC, 2005).
2 For this section, see Kevin Meehan and Paul B. Miller, 'Literature and Popular Culture', in Richard S. Hillman and Thomas D'Agostino, eds, *Understanding the Contemporary Caribbean* (Boulder, CO, 2003), chapter 11,

and O. Nigel Bolland, *The Birth of Caribbean Civilisation: A Century of Ideas about Culture and Identity, Nation and Society* (Oxford and Kingston, Jamaica, 2004).

3 Maurice St Pierre, 'West Indian Cricket as Cultural Resistance', in Michael A. Malec, ed., *The Social Roles of Sport in Caribbean Societies* (Amsterdam, 1995).

4 Pelham Warner, *Long Innings: The Autobiography of Sir Pelham Warner* (London, 1951).

5 Christine Cummings, 'Ideologies of West Indian Cricket', in *The Social Roles of Sport in Caribbean Societies*.

6 Maurice St Pierre, 'West Indian Cricket as Cultural Resistance', in *The Social Roles of Sport in Caribbean Societies*.

7 Alan M. Klein, 'Headcase, Headstrong, and Head-of-the-Class: Resocializing and Labeling in Dominican Baseball', in *The Social Roles of Sport in Caribbean Societies*.

8 Frances Negrón-Muntaner, 'Showing Face: Boxing and Nation Building in Contemporary Puerto Rico', in *Contemporary Caribbean Cultures and Societies*.

9 O. Nigel Bolland, *The Birth of Caribbean Civilisation*, entry on Orlando Patterson.

Chapter 8: Problems and Prospects in the Twenty-first Century

1 Robert B. Potter et al., *The Contemporary Caribbean* (Harlow, Essex, 2004), p. 40.

2 Gregory Knapp, ed., *Latin America in the Twenty-First Century: Challenges and Solutions* (Austin, TX, 2002).

Tables

TABLE 1: COLONIAL ZONES

US ZONE	BRITISH ZONE
US Virgin Islands (St Croix, St Thomas, St John)	Jamaica (1962)
Puerto Rico (politically)	Trinidad and Tobago (1962)
	Barbados (1966)
	Bahamas (1973)
	Grenada (1974)
	Dominica (1978)
HISPANIC ZONE	St Lucia (1979)
	St Vincent (1979)
Cuba (1902)	Antigua-Barbuda (1981)
Dominican Republic (1844)	St Kitts-Nevis (1983)
Puerto Rico (historically and culturally)	Anguilla
	British Virgin Islands
	Cayman Islands
	Montserrat
	Turks and Caicos
NETHERLANDS ZONE	
Aruba	**FRENCH ZONE**
Bonaire	
Curaçao	Haiti (1804)
Saba	Guadeloupe
St Eustatius	Martinique
St Maarten (southern)	St Martin (northern)

Dates indicate year of independence.

TABLE 2: COUNTRIES OF THE CARIBBEAN

COUNTRY	POPULATION ESTIMATE 2005 (MILLIONS)	POPULATION DENSITY PER SQ. MILE	TOTAL AREA (SQ. MILES)	PER CENT URBAN	CAPITAL CITY
Caribbean	39	428	90,653	65	
Antigua-Barbuda	0.1	471	170	37	St John's
Bahamas	0.3	60	5,359	89	Nassau
Barbados	0.3	1,554	166	50	Bridgetown
Cuba	11.3	263	42,803	76	Havana
Dominica	0.1	242	290	71	Roseau
Dominican Republic	8.9	471	18,815	64	Santo Domingo
Grenada	0.1	769	131	39	St George's
Guadeloupe	0.4	681	660	100	Basse-Terre
Haiti	8.3	774	10,714	36	Port-au-Prince
Jamaica	2.7	628	4,243	52	Kingston
Martinique	0.4	935	425	95	Fort-de-France
Netherlands Antilles	0.2	605	309	69	Willemstad
Puerto Rico	3.9	1,132	3,456	94	San Juan
St Kitts-Nevis	0.05	345	139	33	Basseterre
St Lucia	0.2	681	239	30	Castries
St Vincent	0.1	737	150	55	Kingston
Trinidad and Tobago	1.3	659	1,980	74	Port of Spain

Source: Population Reference Bureau, 2005 *World Population Data Sheet* (Washington, DC, 2005)

TABLE 3: CARIBBEAN POPULATION

COUNTRY	2005 POPULATION ESTIMATE (MILLIONS)	BIRTH RATE PER 1,000	DEATH RATE PER 1,000	NATURAL INCREASE (ANNUAL PERCENTAGE)	INFANT MORTALITY RATE PER 1,000 LIVE BIRTHS
Caribbean	39	20	8	1.1	41
Antigua-Barbuda	0.1	20	6	1.4	21
Bahamas	0.3	17	6	1.2	12.7
Barbados	0.3	15	8	0.6	13.2
Cuba	11.3	11	7	0.4	5.8
Dominica	0.1	15	7	0.8	22.2
Dominican Republic	8.9	24	7	1.7	31
Grenada	0.1	19	7	1.2	17
Guadeloupe	0.4	17	7	1.0	6.4
Haiti	8.3	33	14	1.9	80
Jamaica	2.7	19	6	1.3	24
Martinique	0.4	14	8	0.7	8
Netherlands Antilles	0.2	15	8	0.8	9
Puerto Rico	3.9	14	7	0.7	9.8
St Kitts-Nevis	0.05	17	8	1.0	17
St Lucia	0.2	16	6	1.0	14.2
St Vincent	0.1	18	7	1.1	18.1
Trinidad and Tobago	1.3	14	8	0.7	18.6

Source: Population Reference Bureau, 2005 *World Population Data Sheet* (Washington, DC, 2005)

TABLE 4: HUMAN DEVELOPMENT INDEX

HDI RANK HIGH	HDI VALUE 2002	COUNTRY	LIFE EXPECTANCY AT BIRTH 2002	ADULT LITERACY RATE 2002	GDP PER CAPITA (PPP US$) 2002
1	0.956	Norway	78.9	99.0	36,600
4	0.943	Canada	79.3	99.0	29,480
8	0.939	USA	77.0	99.0	35,750
29	0.888	Barbados	77.1	99.7	15,290
39	0.844	St Kitts-Nevis	70.0	97.8	12,420
51	0.815	Bahamas	67.1	95.5	17,280
52	0.809	Cuba	76.7	96.9	5,259
53	0.802	Mexico	73.3	90.5	8,970
54	0.801	Trinidad and Tobago	71.4	98.5	9,430
55	0.800	Antigua-Barbuda	73.9	85.8	10,920
HDI RANK MEDIUM					
71	0.777	St Lucia	72.4	94.8	5,300
79	0.764	Jamaica	75.6	87.6	3,980
87	0.751	St Vincent and The Grenadines	74.0	83.1	5,460
93	0.745	Grenada	65.3	94.4	7,280
95	0.743	Dominica	73.1	76.4	5,640
98	0.738	Dominican Republic	66.7	84.4	6,640
HDI RANK LOW					
153	0.463	Haiti	49.4	51.9	1,610
177	0.273	Sierra Leone	34.3	36.0	520
TERRITORIES NOT IN HDI			Life Expectancy at Birth 2004	Adult Literacy rate 2004	GDP Per capita (PPP US$) 2004
Aruba			79.14	97.0	28,000
Netherlands Antilles			75.83	96.7	11,400
Cayman Islands			79.95	98.0	32,000
Martinique			79.04	97.7	14,400
Puerto Rico			77.62	94.1	17,700

Source: *Human Development Report* (New York, 2004) and www.cia.gov

Selected Further Reading

GENERAL REFERENCE WORKS

Arnold, James, *A History of Literature in the Caribbean*, 3 vols (Amsterdam and Philadelphia, PA, 1994–2001)
Arnold, Peter, *The Illustrated Encyclopedia of World Cricket* (New York, 1986)
Balderston, Daniel, Mike Gonzalez and Ana M. Lopez, eds, *Encyclopedia of Contemporary Latin American and Caribbean Cultures*, 3 vols (London, 2000)
—, *Encyclopedia of Latin American and Caribbean Literature, 1900–2003* (London, 2004)
Davidson, Alan, *The Oxford Companion to Food* (Oxford, 1999)
Mitchell, B.R., *International Historical Statistics: The Americas, 1750–2000*, 5th edn (London, 2003)
Population Reference Bureau, *Population Data Sheet* (Washington, DC, 2005 and 2006)
Shaw, Lisa, and Stephanie Dennison, eds, *Pop Culture in Latin America: Media, Arts and Lifestyles* (Santa Barbara, CA, Denver, CO, and Oxford, 2005)
Statesman's Year-Book (London, 1864–)
West-Duran, Alan, ed., *African Caribbeans: A Reference Guide* (Westport, CT, 2003)

MORE SPECIALIZED WORKS

Alleyne, Mervyn C., *The Construction and Representation of Race and Ethnicity in the Caribbean World* (Kingston, Jamaica, 2002)
Barrow, Christine, and Rhoda Reddock, eds, *Caribbean Sociology: Introductory Readings* (Kingston, Jamaica, 2002)
Barrow-Giles, Cynthia, *Introduction to Caribbean Politics: Text and Readings* (Kingston, Jamaica, 2002)

Beckles, Hilary McD., *A History of Barbados: From Amerindian Settlement to Nation-State* (Cambridge, 1990)
—, and Verene Shepherd, *Caribbean Freedom: Economy and Society from Emancipation to the Present* (Princeton, NJ, 1996)
Blouet, Brian W., and Olwyn M. Blouet, eds, *Latin America and the Caribbean: A Systematic and Regional Survey*, 5th edn (New York, 2006)
Bolland, Nigel O., *The Birth of Caribbean Civilisation: A Century of Ideas about Culture and Identity, Nation and Society* (Kingston, Jamaica, 2004)
Brereton, Bridget, *A History of Modern Trinidad, 1783–1962* (Kingston, Jamaica, 1981)
Bridenbaugh, C., and R. Bridenbaugh, *No Peace Beyond the Line: The English in the Caribbean, 1624–1690* (New York, 1972)
Brown, Judith M., and W. Roger Louis, eds, *The Oxford History of the British Empire: The Twentieth Century* (Oxford, 1999)
Carrington, Selwyn, *The Sugar Industry and the Abolition of the Slave Trade, 1775–1810* (Gainesville, FL, 2002)
Chamberlain, Mary, ed., *Caribbean Migration: Globalized Identities* (London, 1998)
Clarke, Colin, D. Ley and C. Peach, eds, *Geography and Ethnic Pluralism* (London, 1984)
Conway, Dennis, 'Where Is the Environment in Caribbean Development Theory and Praxis?', *Global Development Studies*, III (2002–3), pp. 91–130.
Curtin, Philip, *The Atlantic Slave Trade: A Census* (Madison, WI, 1969)
Desch, Michael C., Jorge I. Dominguez and Andres Serbin, eds, *From Pirates to Drug Lords: The Post-Cold War Caribbean Security Environment* (Albany, NY, 1998)
Dhondy, Farrukh, *C.L.R. James: A Life* (New York, 2001)
Diamond, Jared, *Collapse: How Societies Choose to Fail or Succeed* (New York, 2005)
Downes, A., 'Economic Growth and Development in Barbados during the Twentieth Century', *Integration and Trade Journal*, 15 (2001), pp. 145–76
Drescher, Seymour, *Econocide: British Slavery and the Era of Abolition* (Pittsburgh, PA, 1977)
Drescher, Seymour, and S. Engerman, eds, *A Historical Guide to World Slavery* (Oxford, 1998)
ECLAC (Economic Commission for Latin America and the Caribbean), *Economic Survey of the Caribbean, 2003–2004*, September 2004
Elbow, Gary, 'Regional Cooperation in the Caribbean: The Association of Caribbean States', *Journal of Geography*, 96 (1996), pp. 13–22
Elliott, J. H., *Empires of the Atlantic World: Britain and Spain in America, 1492–1830* (New Haven, CT, and London, 2006)
Eltis, David, *The Rise of African Slavery in the Americas* (Cambridge and New York, 2000)

Ferguson, James, *The Story of the Caribbean People* (Kingston, Jamaica, 1999)
Geggus, David P., *The Impact of the Haitian Revolution in the Atlantic World* (Columbia, SC, 2001)
Gwynne, R. N., and C. Kay, eds, *Latin America Transformed: Globalization and Modernity*, 2nd edn (London, 2004)
Hatchwell, E., and S. Calder, *Cuba: A Guide to the People, Politics and Culture* (New York, 1999)
Heuman, Gad, *The Caribbean: Brief Histories* (Oxford, 2006)
—, and James Walvin, eds, *The Slavery Reader* (London, 2003)
Hey, Jeanne A. K., *Small States in World Politics: Explaining Foreign Policy Behavior* (Boulder, CO, 2003)
Higman, Barry W., *Writing West Indian Histories* (London, 1999)
Hillman R. S., and T. J. D'Agostino, eds, *Understanding the Contemporary Caribbean* (Boulder, CO, and London, 2003)
Hoefte, Rosemarijn, *Connecting Cultures: The Netherlands in Five Centuries of Transatlantic Exchange* (Amsterdam, 1994)
Howard D., *The Dominican Republic: A Guide to the People, Politics and Culture* (New York, 1999)
Human Development Report: Cultural Liberty in Today's Diverse World (New York, 2004)
Klak, Thomas, ed., *Globalization and Neoliberalism: The Caribbean Context* (Lanham, MD, 1998)
Knapp, Gregory, *Latin America in the Twenty-First Century: Challenges and Solutions* (Austin, TX, 2002)
Knight, Franklin W., *The Caribbean: The Genesis of a Fragmented Nationalism*, 2nd edn (New York, 1990)
—, and Teresita Martínez-Vergne, *Contemporary Caribbean Cultures and Societies in a Global Context* (Chapel Hill, NC, 2005)
—, and C. Palmer, eds, *The Modern Caribbean* (Chapel Hill, NC, 1989)
Las Casas, Bartolomé de, *The Devastation of the Indies: A Brief Account*, trans. Herma Briffault (Baltimore, MD, and London, 1992)
Lowenthal, David, *West Indian Societies* (New York, 1972)
Maingot, A.P., and W. Lozano, *The United States and the Caribbean* (New York, 2005)
Malec, Michael A., ed., *The Social Roles of Sport in Caribbean Societies* (Amsterdam, 1995)
Manley, Michael, with Donna Symmonds, *A History of West Indies Cricket* (London, 2002)
McIntosh, Simeon C. R., *Caribbean Constitutional Reform: Rethinking the West Indian Polity* (Kingston, Jamaica, 2002)
Meinig, D. W., *The Shaping of America: A Geographical Perspective on 500 Years of History*, 3 vols (New Haven, CT, 1986)

Miles, Marc, Edwin Feuler and Mary O'Grady, *2005 Index of Economic Freedom*, www.Heritage.org.
Mintz, Sidney W., *Sweetness and Power: The Place of Sugar in World History* (New York, 1986)
Molinelli, J., 'Earthquake Vulnerability Study for the Metropolitan Area of San Juan, Puerto Rico' in D. Barker, ed., *Proceedings of a Meeting of Experts on Hazard Mapping in the Caribbean* (Mona, Jamaica, 1989), pp. 71–86.
Momsen, Janet Henshall, *Gender and Development* (London, 2004)
Moreno Fraginals, M., *Between Slavery and Free Labor: The Spanish-Speaking Caribbean in the Nineteenth Century* (Baltimore, MD, 1985)
Pantin, Denis, *The Caribbean Economy: A Reader* (Kingston, Jamaica, 2005)
Parry, J. H., and P. Sherlock with A. P. Maingot, *A Short History of the West Indies*, 4th edn (London, 1987)
Patterson, Orlando, *Slavery and Social Death: A Comparative Study* (Cambridge, MA, 1982)
Pattulo, Polly, *Last Resorts: The Cost of Tourism in the Caribbean* (Kingston, Jamaica, 1996)
Pérez, Louis A., Jr, *Cuba: Between Reform and Revolution*, 3rd edn (Oxford, 2006)
Pons, Frank Moya, *The Dominican Republic: A National History* (Princeton, NJ, 2005)
Population Reference Bureau, *2005 World Population Data Sheet* (Washington, DC, 2005)
Porter, Andrew, *The Oxford History of the British Empire: The Nineteenth Century* (Oxford, 1999)
Potter, Robert, et al., *The Contemporary Caribbean* (Upper Saddle River, NJ, 2004)
Ramkissoon, 'Explaining Differences in Economic Performance in Caribbean Economies', www.cid.harvard.edu.
—, 'Small Caribbean Economies: What Are We Doing Wrong?', www.cid.harvard.edu.
Ramsaran, R., ed., *Caribbean Survival and the Global Challenge* (Kingston, Jamaica, 2002)
Richardson, Bonham, *The Caribbean in the Wider World* (Cambridge, 1992)
Riddell, B., 'A Tale of Contestation, Disciples and Demands: The Lessons of the Spread of Globalization into Trinidad and Tobago', *Environment and Planning*, 35 (2003), pp. 659–78.
Robertson, R. E. et al., 'Volcano Surveillance and Hazard Mitigation in the Eastern Caribbean', *Caribbean Geography*, 8 (1997), pp. 1–17.
Rogozinski, Jan, *A Brief History of the Caribbean: From the Arawak and Carib to the Present* (New York, 1999)
Shepherd, Verene, ed., *Slavery without Sugar: Diversity in Caribbean Economy and Society since the Seventeenth Century* (Gainesville, FL, 2002)

Sherlock, Philip, and Hazel Bennett, *The Story of the Jamaican People* (Kingston, Jamaica, 1998)

Skelton, T., ed., *Introduction to the Pan-Caribbean* (New York, 2004)

Smith, Frederick, *Caribbean Rum: A Social and Economic History* (Gainesville, FL, 2005)

Stock, Ann-Marie, ed., *Framing Latin American Cinema: Contemporary Critical Perspectives* (Minneapolis, MN, 1997)

Thornton, John, *Africa and Africans in the Making of the Atlantic World* (Cambridge and New York, 1998)

UNESCO *General History of the Caribbean*, 6 vols (London, 1997–9)

Walvin, James, *Atlas of Slavery* (New York, 2006)

Warner, Pelham, *Long Innings: The Autobiography of Sir Pelham Warner* (London, 1951)

Watts, David, *The West Indies: Patterns of Development, Culture and Environmental Change since 1492* (Cambridge, 1987)

West, R., and J. P. Augelli, *Middle America: Its Lands and Peoples* (1966), 3rd edn (Englewood Cliffs, NJ, 1989)

Williams, Eric, *Capitalism and Slavery* (1944) (Chapel Hill, NC, 1994)

World Development Report 2004: Making Services Work for Poor People (Oxford, 2003)

www.joyousjam.com/jamaicahurricanehistory

Acknowledgements

I owe debts to many teachers, researchers and colleagues. West Indian scholars met along the way include Keith Hunte, subsequently Sir Keith, who was welcoming on the University of the West Indies Cave Hill Campus, along with Woodville Marshall. At the Barbados Archives there was help from Michael Chandler and Miss Matthews. The Barbados Museum and Historical Society has given continued support through Alissandra Cummins and Karl Watson. On the Trinidad Campus of the UWI, at a memorable conference in 1988 marking the 150th anniversary of the end of slavery, I enjoyed exchanging ideas with Bridget Brereton, Selwyn Carrington and Carl Campbell, and from the extra-Caribbean contingent: Seymour Drescher, William Green and Mary Turner.

I thank those who taught me at the University of Sheffield and the University of Nebraska. My Nebraska advisor, Lesley Clement Duly, motivated me with his creative mind and nurturing spirit, and steered me to the Caribbean. I learned much on slavery and colonial government from James Rawley and Jack Sosin respectively. I assisted Ben Rader (an excellent tennis player and mixed doubles partner) with the History of Sport course, and Patrice Berger, who supplied a French perspective on the Caribbean. Thanks go to Betty Unterberger, Quincy Adams and Dane Kennedy as colleagues at Texas A&M University. Later, at the College of William & Mary in Virginia, intellectual stimuli came from Bob Gross, Judy Ewell, Cindy Hahamovitch, Ann-Marie Stock, Fredrika Teute, Kris Lane, Dale Hoak, John Selby and Jim McCord.

I have enjoyed three summer seminars funded by the National Endowment for the Humanities, and thank the directors – Joe Miller, Bob Gross, Peter Onuf and Francisco Scarano – and all participants, for memorable insights and meetings in Charlottesville, Williamsburg and Madison. Professor Kenneth Kirkwood invited me to participate in his Racial and Ethnic Studies Seminar at St Anthony's College, Oxford, which was a stimulating experience.

At Virginia State University I have received generous support from everyone, and a research leave to complete *The Contemporary Caribbean*. Thank you Dean Weldon Hill, Provost Eric Thomas and President Eddie N. Moore Jr. Joe Goldenberg, Chair of History and Philosophy at VSU for many years, was always enlightening and encouraging, and his successor, Arthur Abraham, has added a West African dimension to my views of the Caribbean. Other colleagues who have been cheerily supportive are Renée Hill, Dirk Philipsen, Shelia Lassiter, Wesley Hogan, Majid Amini, Paul Alkebulan, Christina Proenza-Coles, Richard Chew, Hilde Rissel, Carl Garrott and Consuelo Navarro. Sarah Bundy has given invaluable technical advice. To all: thank you.

Finally, thanks go to my husband, Brian W. Blouet, who has given time, knowledge, energy and enthusiasm throughout this project.

Copyright Acknowledgements

Index